Nina Talmén

Special Skills in International Adoptive Parenting

Nina Talmén

# Special Skills in International Adoptive Parenting

Case Study of Five Finnish International Adoptive Parents

VDM Verlag Dr. Müller

## Imprint

Bibliographic information by the German National Library: The German National Library lists this publication at the German National Bibliography; detailed bibliographic information is available on the Internet at http://dnb.d-nb.de.

Any brand names and product names mentioned in this book are subject to trademark, brand or patent protection and are trademarks or registered trademarks of their respective holders. The use of brand names, product names, common names, trade names, product descriptions etc. even without a particular marking in this works is in no way to be construed to mean that such names may be regarded as unrestricted in respect of trademark and brand protection legislation and could thus be used by anyone.

Cover image: www.purestockx.com

Publisher:
VDM Verlag Dr. Müller Aktiengesellschaft & Co. KG , Dudweiler Landstr. 125 a, 66123 Saarbrücken, Germany,
Phone +49 681 9100-698, Fax +49 681 9100-988,
Email: info@vdm-verlag.de

Zugl.: Jyväskylä, University of Jyväskylä, 2007

Copyright © 2008 VDM Verlag Dr. Müller Aktiengesellschaft & Co. KG and licensors
All rights reserved. Saarbrücken 2008

Produced in USA and UK by:
Lightning Source Inc., La Vergne, Tennessee, USA
Lightning Source UK Ltd., Milton Keynes, UK
BookSurge LLC, 5341 Dorchester Road, Suite 16, North Charleston, SC 29418, USA

**ISBN: 978-3-639-02891-1**

**TABLE OF CONTENTS**

1. INTRODUCTION ............................................................................................................... 2
2. IDENTITY ......................................................................................................................... 4
   2.1 The Development of Identity .................................................................................... 5
   2.2 Adoptive Parents, Adopted Children and Identity ................................................... 7
3. BEING ADOPTIVE PARENT ......................................................................................... 10
   3.1 Ethnic Awareness ..................................................................................................... 11
      3.1.1 Vonk's 12 Recommendations Concerning Ethnic Awareness ...................... 12
   3.2 Multicultural Planning .............................................................................................. 12
      3.2.1 Vonk's 14 Recommendations Concerning Multicultural Planning .............. 14
   3.3 Survival Skills ........................................................................................................... 15
      3.3.1 Vonk's 13 Recommendations Concerning Survival Skills ........................... 16
   3.4 Cultural Socialization ............................................................................................... 16
      3.4.1 Cultural assimilation ......................................................................................... 17
      3.4.2 Enculturation ..................................................................................................... 18
      3.4.3 Ethnic Inculcation ............................................................................................. 18
      3.4.4 Child Choice ...................................................................................................... 19
4. INTERNATIONAL ADOPTION IN FINLAND ............................................................ 20
   4.1 The International Adoption Process in Finland ..................................................... 22
5. DESCRIPTION OF THE RESEARCH PROCESS ......................................................... 25
   5.1 The Aim of the Research and the Research Question ........................................... 26
   5.2 Conducting the Research ......................................................................................... 26
   5.3 Description of the Interview Data ........................................................................... 29
6. RESULTS ......................................................................................................................... 31
   6.1 About the Different Ethnic Backgrounds ............................................................... 34
   6.2 Special Skills in International Adoptive Parenting ................................................ 39
   6.3 Child's Birth Country in Everyday Life .................................................................. 43
   6.4 About the Identity ..................................................................................................... 47
   6.5 Issues of Racism ....................................................................................................... 53
   7.1 Guiding Half-Enculturation ..................................................................................... 63
   7.2 International Adoptive Parents' Special Skills ....................................................... 65
   7.3 Discussion and Evaluation of the Study ................................................................. 66
BIBLIOGRAPHY: ................................................................................................................ 68
APPENDIX 1 ........................................................................................................................ 74

1. INTRODUCTION

International adoption is a way of starting a family by legally joining parents and children from different countries together. It has during the last 30 years become part of our everyday lives. 338 children were adopted from abroad to Finland in the year 2005, and 310 children in the year 2004. The amount of international adoptions has been growing all the time during the last 20 years, starting from 1985. (Tilastokeskus 2006.) The previous researches (e.g. Yoon 2001) have proved that good international adoptive parenting can prevent adopted persons' mental and behavioural promlems. Haimi-Kaikkonen (2007: 6) and associates state that "Adoptive parenthood is a special parenthood that is not directly comparable to biological parenthood. Good adoptive parenthood implies understanding and flexibility; mental and physical ability to meet adoptive child's special needs in his/her all phases of life". Adoptive parents of children from different ethnic background than their own must, in addition, have certain kind of skills in order to meet their children's unique ethnic and cultural needs (Vonk 2001: 248). Besides the growth of the number of adoptions, the present study is important from the point of society: through undesrstanding what these skills are, it can help the future adoptive parents to gain these particular skills and become better adoptive parents.

Pitkänen (2000) has examined international adoptive parents in Finland in her pro gradu thesis. Her study consists of 140 families who filled in a multiple choice and open answer questionnaire that was mailed to them. The result of Pitkänen's study was, that the adoptive parents said, that it is important to support their children's ethnic identity, thus it would help them to grow with healthy self esteem. Most of the parents in Pitkänen's study took part of their children's birth culture to the side of families Finnish culture, and used other various ways to support it. Because of Pitkänen's findings it is clear that Finnish adoptive families are making an effort in supporting their children's ethnic identities, and for that reason must include in their lives different kinds of activities that biological families do not have to. In the present study I want to understand how they are prepared to such mission and what special skills they feel they need in adoptive parenthood.

As a journalist I have written articles about international adoption. This has awakened a personal interest to the subject and to the stories behind these normal, but still different families. When I begun my studies in the Master's Program in Intercultural Communication, I realized that it could give me a possibility to learn more about the subject academically. The aim of the present study is to understand international adoption in Finland, and what is associated to that phenomenon. I chose to limit the point of view of this study in understanding what kind of special skills related to parenting an internationally adopted child are needed. I defined the subject even more by concentrating to the five Finnish adoptive parents represented in this research: what are the skills they do consider important. This does not mean the everyday skills all parents need in child care, but the skills that are needed especially in living with a child from different ethnic background than the parents themselves are.

In this research I will first present the identity development processes in order to explain the importance of international adoptive parents' actions in their children's identity development. Then I will present Lee's (2003) cultural socialization theory that he has modulated particularly to international adoptive families. Vonk (2001) has, from the basis of earlier adoption studies, developed a model that shows in which areas international adoptive parents need to focus and gain skills, knowledge and awareness in, so that they can develop their own cultural competence. Because these kinds of studies have been made with adoptive families in the United States, it is important to research Finnish international adoptive parents as well to see how these results look in the Finnish context. I chose these two theories (Vonk's & Lee's) because one of them alone could not conclusively explain the researched phenomenon. I try to find an answer for my research question by half-structured theme interview. As a basic and flexible method, it is the best choice for discussing about intimate family matters.

## 2. IDENTITY

The earlier studies in Finland (e.g. Pitkänen 2000, Pärssinen-Hentula, 1993) and abroad (e.g. Yoon 2001, DeBerry et al. 1996) have risen up the importance of identity in the discussion of international adoption. *Identity* can be defined as something that an individual believes he or her is – who he/she is. It changes during the years: identity is always in process. (Hall 1999: 223; Van Gulden & Bartels-Rabb 2005: 57) "Identity is changeable because it is in part formed in response to one's roles, environment, and significant others, all of which can vary throughout life" (Van Gulden & Bartels-Rabb 2005: 57). G. G. Harris's (1989 cited in Seelye & Wasilewski 1996) has defined The Three Faces of Me. First of all there is the *Biological Me* that means the physical individual. This realization of being a separate creature has begun already billions of years ago among the cells, and it develops early in human childhood. The *Conscious Me* is something added to the chemical and biological parts of person. This core-self "allows us to experience a feeling of coherence, of continuing identity" (Seelye & Wasilewski 1996: 105). The *Me in Society* aspect needs social affirmation. The way we contact the others and maintain relationships is influenced by the collective wisdom of culture. (Seelye & Wasilewski 1996: 103) Tajfel and Turner have created *Social Identity Theory*. According to it, in addition to personal identity, we also form an identity for a particular group, and also get the parts of the building blocks of the identity from this group. In order to enhance the sense of identity we make comparisons with out-groups. This also includes power relations. "(…) the greater is the relative power of a group, the more secure will it feel in its ascendance (…)" Tajfel 1982: 489).

*Cultural identity* is a developed selfhood that is connected to individuals culture. It helps to differentiate "we and the others". (Kim 2001: 48-49.) Cultural identity also highlights the cultural codes and common historical experiences that make people to feel as one nation (Hall 199: 224). Related to cultural identity, Seelye and Wasilewski (1996) have a good example of a Japanese young man who was raised in France. He had Japanese parents and had always felt like Japanese, but when he travelled to Japan at the age of 18, the local people considered him outsider. (Seelye & Wasilewski 1996: 102.) Adopted children have many times same kind of experiences when they visit the country they were born in: even they look the same as the locals, their upbringing is a result of different culture. For that reason they behave differently, and do feel outsiders in their birth country. Pärssinen-Hentula (1993) has examined what is internationally adopted children's relation to their birth countries. In her study, based on interviews of 25 seven to twelve years old children and their parents, she noticed that the adopted children had elements of double identity. Pärssinen-Hentula's study also reveals that the parents are important link to internationally adopted children's birth countries.

*Bicultural* person was first called in the sociological literature *dual-culture personality*. Park's (1928) term was *"marginal" man*, because that kind of person has, for some of the numerous reasons, left one culture but could not have adjusted to another. The idea of marginality is still present in contemporary studies. Del Pilar and Udasco (2004: 11) state: "Being caught between cultures frequently does result in difficulties and adjustment problems". Some researches anyhow see that being part of two cultures does not necessarily mean that there has to be a psychological conflict. "In this bicultural perspective, the person does not favour one culture over the other. And more often than not, the dual transmission of cultural information from parents and other caretakers is quite deliberate and both cultures are presented positively". (Padilla 2006: 470.) If a person is really biculturally competent, he or she can easily switch from one culture to another, and still be like a native. This person has two social personas and identities. That makes him or her usually more competent, even in the interaction with people who come from totally different cultures than the ones that the person manages. (Padilla 2006: 471.)

2.1 The Development of Identity

Van Gulden & Bartels-Rabb (2005: 57) state that "Identity formation is a complex equation of inputs and outputs where neither side of the equation alone provides a complete explanation for the individual's chosen identity. Rather, what the person takes in from others and what he puts out in response combine to determine who that individual is".

In her study Mikkola (2001) concentrates on the development of immigrant school children's multicultural identity, but I believe that her theory (the development of bicultural identity) can be applied to adopted children as well, because the inputs presented in Table 1 are similar for international adoptive children's bicultural identity development.

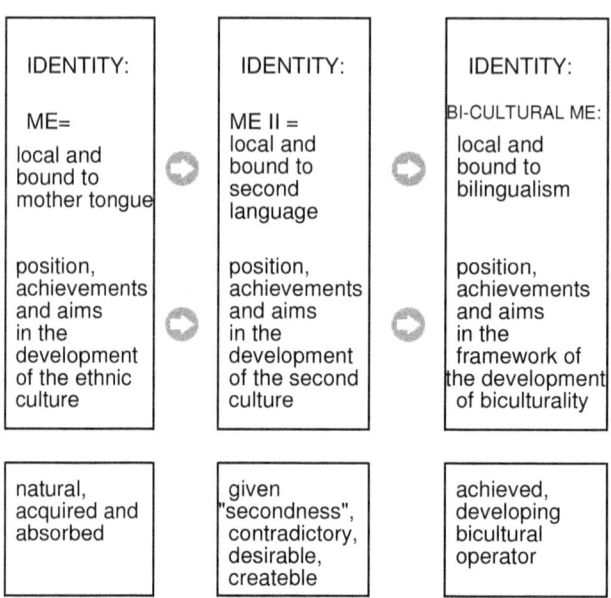

Table 1. The development of bicultural identity (translated from Mikkola 2001: 121)

Mikkola has in her research studied 26 immigrant children. The participants came from six ethnic backgrounds. They were pupils of two elementary schools situated in the South-West-Finland. As informants she had 56 immigrants and same amount of Finnish fifth and sixth grade students and 14 teachers. Mikkola conducted her study, which was combination of qualitative and quantitative research, by interviews and surveys. The surveys were filled in the presence of researcher. (2001: 123.) "Reports of the groups do not offer easy access for the reader because their interpretation has been left open" Mikkola describes the results (2001: 223).

Mikkola found out that ethnicity illuminates from inside, and that identity is the product of culture and it is built in communication (Mikkola 2001: 223, 225, 231). She presents in her theory that the bicultural identity develops on the basis of ethnic culture, and by learning the second culture. The identity of second culture takes form from the communication positions that the individual has in the context culture. (Mikkola 2001: 121.) The representatives of each culture can support the features of their own culture in child's "me" but the child has to do the integration (of these two cultures) him/herself (Mikkola 2001: 119). Mikkola states that the pupil has to accept the both cultural dimensions in him/her in order to develop positive biculturalism. If the ethnicity is never mentioned, its social status decreases, and it can be hidden. Many pupils, however, found it pleasant to discuss about the ethnicity in the research interviews. (Mikkola 2001: 227) Kerwin and associates (1993) had also interesting results in their study of "Black/White" families. They found out that "cohesive biracial [bicultural] identity is possible and that young children naturally view themselves as biracial [bicultural] if they are exposed to both cultures and their parents foster an open dialogue on the topic" (Friedlander et al. 2000: 188).

2.2 Adoptive Parents, Adopted Children and Identity

Identity is usually associated with genetic and ethnic identity, but even the children that are adopted from the same culture and/or ethnic heritage struggle with identity formation. (Van Gulden & Bartels-Rabb 2005: 54) "It's not surprising (…) that at one time or another most adopted children entertain the possibility that something they did or something about themselves caused their birth parents to choose not to raise them" (Van Gulden & Bartels-Rabb 2005: 54). This feeling of abandonment may cause a risk that the adopted child develops so called *shame-based identity*. "If the child blames herself and is unable to resolve these feelings, accepting the thought as a fact and incorporating the resulting implications into her identity, she is likely to develop shame-based identity." (Van Gulden & Bartels-Rabb 2005: 55). There have been contradictory results in the research about international adoptees psychological adjustment. Some studies show that even 70 - 80 percent of these adoptees have some serious behavioural and emotional problems, whereas other studies state that there is only few, if none, differences when comparing same ethnicity (with adoptive parents) adoptees and/or non-adoptees. (Lee 2003: 716.) Lee (2003: 717) complains in his ethnic identity research review that "(…) the actual relationship between the racial and the ethnic experiences of transracial [international] adoptees and their psychological adjustments is not directly addressed in the studies. In addition, none of the studies used reliable and valid measures of racial/ethnic identity." Hollingsworth (1997) found out in her study that "transracial [international] adoptees had significantly lower racial/ethnic identities than same race-adoptees" (Lee 2003: 717). This result correlated to other research that showed high acculturation to majority culture for domestic and international adoptees (Lee 2003: 717). Generally speaking it can be said that the studies listed in Lee's article show mixed results considering adoptees ethnic identity development.

Adoptive parents can possibly prevent the shame-based identity development by accepting their child's feelings, but not supporting his or her idea about that his or her expression of herself/himself is true. Like there is a struggle in identity formation, there is also conflict between the cultures, even if the child comes from the same ethnic heritage as his or her parents. (Van Gulden & Bartels-Rabb 2005: 55.) "The older the child is at time of placement, the more poignant the cultural contradictions are likely to be for him" (Van Gulden & Bartels-Rabb 2005: 55). Wickes & Slate (1996) had research results that international adoptees, which were placed to their new home and parents in later age, identified more strongly with their ethnicities than those who were placed younger. These results correspond to Virkki's (2006: 12) similar findings of the subject: "a young woman who was adopted to Finland when she was already six years old identified more closely to her native country than an adoptee who arrived when he/she was a baby." In Finland, however, most internationally adopted children are under three years old (see Table 2).

| Child's age when adopted | Amount of children |
|---|---|
| Under 1 year | 663 |
| 1 year old | 667 |
| 2 years old | 420 |
| 3 years old | 240 |
| 4 years old | 179 |
| 5 years old | 149 |
| Over 6 years old | 280 |
| Total | 2598 |

Table 2. Internationally adopted children's amount during the years 1985-2004 classified by age (Suomen kansainvälisten lapseksiottamisasioiden lautakunta 2005: 17).

Lee (2003: 718-719) summarizes in his article some points in international adoptees ethnic identity development. 1) It may vary according to the social and emotional development of the children. For example, measured by ethnic preference Lee remarks studies that show that younger children tend to identify ethnically with their birth cultures whereas sometimes adoptees' sense of ethnicity becomes more ambivalent or diminishes when they reach adolescence and adulthood. 2) There is however opposite results as well: Freundlich & Lieberthal (2000) found out that 36 % Korean adoptees described themselves as Caucasian when they were growing up (42% described themselves as Korean/Asian) but only 11% thought so when they were adults (and 78% were now identified as Korean/Asian). 3) It is also researched that if international adoptees live in ethnically homogenous communities their ethnic identity appears to be weaker.

This subject has not been abundantly researched in Finland, but for example Virkki (2006) studied the cultural identity and experiences of feeling different in her pro gradu thesis. She interviewed 11 internationally adopted young persons. She also investigated how adoptees' native country could be seen in his/her life and how they felt about Finnishness (Virkki 2006: 12). All the people interviewed in Virkki's study perceived themselves primarily as Finns. Still she states that they could be easily divided to two groups: in those who felt completely Finns and in those who felt that the identity of their native country was shown in their identity. (Virkki 2006: 12.) But whatever identity these young adoptees had, they felt that "(…) they have to behave two times better than other people in their age, and through that also be two times more hardworking to be accepted among the majority" (Virkki 2006: 12).

Yoon's (2001) study showed that "Korean adolescent adoptees, whose adoptive parents actively promoted their children's ethnic cultures, had more positive racial/ethnic identity development, and in turn, better psychological adjustment" (Lee 2003: 720). Still sometimes the adoptees themselves may rather identify with the majority culture and reject their parents' efforts (Freundlich & Lieberthal, 2000). They can also develop more flexibility identity, which can be bicultural or otherwise fluid and across the cultural borders giving (Lee 2003: 722). Interesting fact about parents' behaviour in their adopted children's ethnic identity development comes out in DeBerry and associates' (1996) research. "Nearly half of all adoptive parents were likely to encourage biculturalism in the upbringing of their children during childhood, but (…) were more likely to deny and deemphasize race (…) when their children reached adolescent" (Lee 2003: 720). I described here why it is important that the international adoptive parents understand that their role in their children's identity development is crucial. When the child is young, his or her parents are the only link to their birth country. In the next chapter I will discuss how the adoptive parents could practically help their children in their identity development, and what kind of challenges it brings to be an adoptive parent.

## 3. BEING ADOPTIVE PARENT

Adoptive parents of children from different ethnic background than their own must develop a certain kind of a competence in order to meet their children's unique ethnic and cultural needs. This process of developing the competence can be long and engaging. (Vonk 2001: 248.) Vonk (2001: 249) has, from the base of earlier adoption studies, developed a model that shows in which areas transracial [international] adoptive parents need to focus and gain skills, knowledge and awareness in, so that they can develop their cultural competence. These three areas are: 1) *Racial Awareness* [in this research *Ethnic Awareness*], 2) *Multicultural Planning*, and 3) *Survival Skills*. She has also identified, with eight adoption professionals, recommendations to each area that adoptive families should take into account, recommendable already while receiving adoption counselling. (Vonk 2001: 252-254.) I use these as tools to investigate what kind of special skills, related to parenting an internationally adopted child, the Finnish parents feel they need. I formed the half-structured theme interview from these themes and questions (Appendix 1).

I first introduce one by one the areas in which Vonk states that the international adoptive parents should have special skills in, and then after, her recommendations concerning every area. She has chosen "I" to start every recommendations with, because she thinks that it is active and accurate representation of parental cultural competence (Vonk 2001: 252). For this research I have changed the term race for ethnic in Vonk's recommendations and in all the other theories. Also the form of adoption I discuss in this study is *international adoption*, even the theories I quote use the term of *transracial adoption* with the definition of "joining of racially different parents and children together in adoptive families" (Silverman 1993: 104) or "it generally refers to the adoption of black or biracial children by white adoptive families, although the term properly refers to any adoption across racial or ethnic lines" (Encyclopedia of Adoption 2000). In Finland this term is, however, not preferred, and it is hardly ever used here anywhere.

Uhtio (2006: 42) describes in her article the problem of finding suitable word/words to describe international adoptive families in Finland. "American terms transracial adoption and interracial family just do not fit the Finnish language" she states. These terms do not fit in the common Finnish cultural way of thinking either. There has been a discussion going on if the term *multicultural family* would be best to use - at least so far before someone comes up with a better idea (Uhtio 2006: 42). "On the other hand, someone has said that his/her family is multicultural characteristically in his/her criteria only because of the fact that their children have born in some other country" (Uhtio 2006: 42). Friedlander and associates (2000) stated in their study that most parents construed their family as whole multiculturally (e.g. Brazilian American family), and this "not only reflects the family's cultural transition but also serves to reduce the children's sense of isolation or differentness" (2000: 196). Still parents could also call their family "a mishmash", that reflected diversity and "identify their children by their children's birth heritage (e.g. 'Korean' or 'Paraguayan')" (Friedlander et al. 2000: 192). In this research I use the term international adoption when I refer to Finnish adoptive parents and their adopted children who come from different ethnic backgrounds.

3.1 Ethnic Awareness

The first area pays attention to the fact that international adoptive parents should be ethnically aware. And this does not only mean their children's ethnicity but their own as well. The importance of thinking ones own ethnicity raises from the fact that, as referred later in this study, adoptive parents have usually taken their ethnicity for granted without necessity to really think about it. (Vonk 2001: 249-250.) *White benefits* (Kivel 1998) are a good example of this, even the terminology does not feel suitable for Finnish people. White benefits are invisible to those who have them, but they are existing advantages based on race [ethnicity]. Vonk (2001: 249) also reminds the importance of understanding the fact that racism and discrimination really do exist. Parents' should also take into consideration that their culture and its features should not be defined as normal. Doing so can be result of lack of meeting people from other cultures, which can lead to ethnocentrism, that may cause difficulties to understand what kind of difficulties children from different ethnic background can face from the side of majority. (Vonk 2001: 249-250.) "The [international adoptive] families are forever interracial and, as such, are not immune to having prejudice or racism directed toward them or toward their children" (Vonk 2001: 250). That is why parents should also honestly observe their own possible prejudice towards their adoptive children's culture so that they could be "aware of their own blind spots to help their children develop pride in their racial [ethnic] identities" (Vonk 2001: 250).

### 3.1.1 Vonk's 12 Recommendations Concerning Ethnic Awareness

1. I understand how my own cultural background influences the way I think, act, and speak.
2. I am able to recognize my own ethnic prejudice.
3. I am aware of stereotypes and preconceived notions that I may hold toward other ethnic minority groups.
4. I have examined my feelings and attitudes about the birth culture and ethnicity of my children.
5. I make ongoing efforts to change my own prejudiced attitudes.
6. I have thoroughly examined my motivation for adopting a child of a different ethnicity or culture than myself.
7. I am knowledgeable of and continue to develop respect for the history and culture of my children's ethnic heritage.
8. I understand the unique needs of my child related to his or her ethnic or cultural status.
9. I know that international-cultural adoptive parenting involves extra responsibilities over and above those of biological parenting.
10. I have examined my feelings about interethnic dating and marriage.
11. I know that others may view my family as "different".
12. I know that my children may be treated unkindly or unfairly because of racism.

(Vonk 2001: 252)

### 3.2 Multicultural Planning

Multicultural planning is a tool for parents to help their adopted children to develop their ethnic identity. It "refers to the creation of avenues for the internationally adopted child to learn about and participate in his or her culture of birth" (Vonk 2001: 251). There are findings that show that Finnish international adoptive parents are active in supporting their children's identity development (Pitkänen 2000). Vonk (2001) emphasizes that children living in adoptive families, and probably even in ethnically heterogenic neighbourhood, should have some contacts with people of their own ethnic background in order to build pride in their ethnicity, and/or birth culture. Even if the parents themselves have some methods to involve in children's birth culture (for example reading about it and visiting families from that country), Steinberg and Hall (1998 cited in Vonk 2001: 251) stated that international adoptive parents "cannot themselves teach their children about a culture to which they themselves do not belong; they must instead help their children find role models within their birth cultures". Friedlander and associates found out what was most of times the reason for parents choosing particular country of adoption: the country itself and the people living in that particular country just felt comfortable for them. Other common reason was that family had already adopted child/children from that country before. (Friedlander et al. 2000: 191-192.)

Friedlander and associates (2000) investigated internationally adopted children and their parents in the United States. They conducted interviews of 8 adoptive families about bicultural identification. They found out that most families celebrated their children's heritage by attending support groups that were specialized to that. But there were also ways of doing that in home "In addition to visiting museums and participating in cultural events, parents actively bring the child's culture into the home in a variety of ways, including food, music, dance, and holidays. They make efforts to create ties with students or adults from the child's country of origin, and they have friends or acquaintances from that country or other countries. (Friedlander et al. 2000: 192)". Visiting children's birth country with their children was also on most of the families "to do" -list if they have not already done so (Friedlander et al. 2000: 192).

DeBerry and associates (1996) found out in their research with 88 African American adoptees that if the parents of these adoptees promoted actively their children's ethnicities (e.g. learned about African American heritage), the adoptees had more positive ethnic identity development. It also correlated with more positive adjustment. Yoon's (2001) study showed similar results with Korean adolescent adoptees. They had also more positive ethnic identity development, if their parents promoted actively adoptees' ethnic cultures. This led, as well, to better psychological adjustment. Huh (1997: 85) suggested that parents' involvement and enthusiasm about their adopted children's culture of birth affected the way that the children became more interested and comfortable as well. These results show that it is also important to Finnish parents to support their children's ethnicity.

The findings of Friedlander and associates (2000) research showed that all the children that were interviewed identified with Euro-American culture (their parents' culture) but still labelled themselves ethnically. "There was little evidence of identity confusion and little reported pressure to choose one identity over the other" (Friedlander et al. 2000: 196). On that basis Friedlander and associates stated that there is a difference between cultural identification and ethnic identification, even though those terms have been commonly used as synonyms in literature. Friedlander and associates (2000: 196) clarified their findings by defining *cultural identification* as "having a sense of shared customs, attitudes, and values within a particular group", and *ethnic identification* as "to viewing oneself as a member of a national or regional (e.g. Latin American) group". Parents in Friedlander and associates (2000) research considered important that their children feel pride in their birth heritage, and the parents also tried to promote their cultural identification by "acknowledging their children's physical differences and emphasizing their psychological similarities" (Friedlander et al. 2000: 196).

Lee (2003: 711-712) states that so called *transracial adoption paradox* [in this research referred as *international adoption paradox*] takes form when parents adopt children that are considered ethnic minorities in the receiving country. This adoption can be either domestic or international, but in Finland's case it is most likely international. "Namely, adoptees are ethnic minorities in society, but they are perceived and treated by others, and sometimes themselves, as if they are members of the majority culture due to adoption into a White family", Lee (2003: 711) explains the international adoption paradox, which I will discuss more carefully later in this study.

3.2.1 Vonk's 14 Recommendations Concerning Multicultural Planning

1. I include regular contact with people of other ethnicities and cultures in my life.
2. I place my children in multicultural schools.
3. I place my children with teachers who are ethnically aware and skilled with children of my child's ethnicity.
4. I understand how my choices about where to live affect my child.
5. I have developed friendships with families and individuals of colour who are good role models for my children.
6. I purchase books, toys, and dolls that are like my child.
7. I include traditions from my child's birth culture in my family celebrations.
8. I provide my children with opportunities to establish relationships with adults from their birth culture.

9. I provide my children with the opportunity to learn the language of their birth culture.
10. I provide my children with the opportunity to appreciate the music of their birth culture.
11. I have visited the country or community of my child's birth.
12. I have demonstrated the ability for sustained contact with members of my child's ethnic group.
13. I seek services and personal contacts in the community that will support my child's ethnicity.
14. I live in a community that provides my child with same-ethnicity adult and peer role models on an ongoing basis.

(Vonk 2001: 253)


3.3 Survival Skills

Adoptive parents may not have experience of racism that has been expressed toward them. Still international adoptive parents should be able to help their children to cope with discrimination and racism. (Vonk 2001: 251.) "(...) it is not possible to protect children from racism, [but] it is possible to help them actively cope with it" (Vonk 2001: 251). Good ways of doing that are exchanging thoughts with families with same experiences, and talking about the subject in home, not downplaying it. (Vonk 2001: 251.)

Cederblad and associates (1999: 1242-1247) conducted a study of 211 internationally adopted young people in Sweden. The geographical closeness and societies' similarities make these results interesting regarding my study. They found out that adoptees had lower self-esteem and more behavioural problems if they had faced negative ethnic experiences. In that situation even the support of family and friends did not help to ease these symptoms. There are also other studies that support that fact (Lee 2003: 719). Vice versa, positive racial and ethnic experiences affect the adoptees just the opposite way (Lee 2003: 720). The couple of young Finnish adoptees themselves pointed out that "the most important thing is to which nationality you yourself identify with. But when it is a question of getting the 'acceptance' of an outsider, the importance of outward appearance is being emphasized." (Virkki 2006: 13)

3.3.1 Vonk's 13 Recommendations Concerning Survival Skills

1. I educate my children about the realities of racism and discrimination.
2. I help my children cope with racism through open and honest discussion in our home about race and oppression.
3. I am aware of the attitudes of friends and family members toward my child's ethnic and cultural differences.
4. I am aware of variety of strategies that can be used to help my child cope with acts of prejudice or racism.
5. I know how to handle unique situations, such as my child's attempts to alter his or her physical appearance to look more like family members or friends.
6. I help my children recognize racism.
7. I help my children develop pride in them selves.
8. I tolerate no biased remarks about any group of people.
9. I seek peer support to counter frustration resulting from overt and covert acts of racism toward my children, my family, or me.
10. I seek support and guidance from others who have a personal understanding of racism, particularly those from my child's ethnicity or birth culture.
11. I have acquired practical information about how to deal with insensitive questions from strangers.
12. I help my children understand that being discriminated against does not reflect personal shortcomings.
13. I am able to validate my children's feelings, including anger and hurt related to racism and discrimination.

(Vonk 2001: 253)

3.4 Cultural Socialization

*Cultural socialization* is a developmental process that takes a whole lifetime. It creates the transmission of cultural values, customs and believes especially for the ethnic minorities. Behaviours transmitted from friends, family, parents, and community to children foster ethnic identity development. They as well equip children with coping strategies to deal with racism and discrimination, and encourage pro-social behaviour and appropriate participation in society. (Lee 2003: 720-721.) In the families where adopted children represent different ethnicity [the adoption is international] cultural socialization process is complicated because there are ethnic differences between parents and children. That forms the basis of international adoption paradox. There is also a problem that, adoptive parents that represent different ethnicity than their adopted children, may not be able to teach their children how the life as ethnic minorities in the society, because they may not have the first hand knowledge about it. (Lee 2003: 721.)

Lee (2003) has summarized four *cultural socialization strategies* by modifying them from the traditional views to suit better to international adoptive families. In these classifications the unique ethnic dynamics within these families have been taken into account. These strategies "characterize typical ways in which transracial [international] adoptive families (specifically, parents and children) might approach the transracial [international] adoption paradox" (Lee 2003: 721). They include *Cultural assimilation, Enculturation, Racial inculcation*, and *Child choice*. Lee explains, however, that these classifications are not exhaustive, and that there can be many other strategies to resolve the international adoption paradox (2003: 723). I present these strategies in the following chapters as I use them in the present research when analyzing my findings.

3.4.1 Cultural assimilation

Cultural assimilation is a strategy where parents need to make very little effort. Children are instantly and continually "exposed to the majority culture". Sometimes parents even refuse to see any ethnic differences in their children. This strategy is considered to be so called colour-blind. (Lee 2003: 721.) This refers straight to Vonk's demand on parents' ethnic awareness: if the parents are not ethnically aware, they are likely to use cultural assimilation strategy. Early studies done in The United States, considering the international adoptions in the country, revealed that most parents preferred to raise their adopted children paying no special attention to their ethnic differences or unique experiences related to them (Anduio, 1998; DeBerry et al., 1996; McRoy and Zurcher, 1983). Parents' aim was to acculturate the child to the majority culture. McRoy and Zurcher (1983) claim that internationally adopted children who experience this kind of a cultural assimilation "are more likely to internalize their adoptive parents' cultural worldview and identify more strongly with the majority culture than with their ethnic cultures" (Lee 2003: 721).

### 3.4.2 Enculturation

Recent research shows that more and more adoptive parents are ethnically aware and want to enculturate their children. They understand that there are differences within their family compared to biological ones. These parents "typically provide their children with educational, social, and cultural opportunities to instil ethnic awareness, knowledge, pride, values, and behaviours, as to promote a positive ethnic identity" (Lee 2003: 722). Silverman (1983), and Huh and Reid (2000) reported that when the parents of internationally adopted children promoted ethnic participation for their children, lived in the area with residents of different ethnicities, brought out their children's ethnic roots, and took part in these activities with their children, adoptees were more like to show pride of their ethnicity. These all parents' actions fit in the recommendations Vonk has for ethnically aware parents.

### 3.4.3 Ethnic Inculcation

Adoptive parents adopt different attitudes towards ethnic issues. There is, however, not much empirical research that would show the level of commitment that the parents show in teaching their children coping skills to deal effectively with discrimination and racism or engage in racial [here ethnic] inculcation. (Lee 2003: 722.) Andujo (1988), Friedlander and associates (2000), and Johnson and associates (1987), found out in their studies that "parents may downplay racist comments, make derogatory comments about racists, and in fewer cases, take more active role in the community to promote social justice" (Lee 2003: 722). Also Friedlander and associates (2000: 192) found signs of parents more active role in community by stating that "[In order to relate to their children's birth culture] some [parents] have been actively involved in promoting diversity in their children's schools."

Friedlander and associates (2000: 194) had quite similar findings in their research. The parents they interview told that they used numeral methods to help their children to cope. These parents fostered pride in their children's heritage, attended support groups, and considered carefully how to discuss prejudice with their children. Some parents also believe that enculturation is a good way to prepare children to face discrimination and racism (Steinberg and Hall, 2000). Parents in favour of racial inculcation "were slightly more likely to read books and attend cultural events that focused on the promotion of a positive ethnic identity than a positive racial identity" (Westues & Cohen 1998 cited in Lee 2003: 722). These ideas complete survival skills' part of Vonks model.

3.4.4 Child Choice

This fourth socialization strategy has emerged in recent years (Tessler et al. 1999). In this strategy parents let the children decide if they want to make use of the cultural opportunities the parents are providing them. Tessler and associates did not anyhow present any empirical support to their strategy, but just some anecdotal examples (Lee 2003: 723). In child choice parents burden their children with the responsibility of deciding what they should do in the means of getting raised. That can lead to a point where children became interested in their ethnic cultures only to please their parents. (Lee 2003: 723.) DeBerry and associates (1996) discovered in their study of African American adoptees that "many adoptive parents become more ambivalent about engaging in cultural socialization when their children entered adolescence, possibly because the children became less interested or the parents became more uncomfortable" (Lee 2003: 723). Friedlander and associates (2000: 192) noticed that "Most parents expect that their children's self-identification with the birth culture will grow stronger with age, and parents of older children have already noticed this change."

This chapter 3 presented the findings that Lee and Vonk had brought up. I will discuss later how these theories have affected to the formation of my research question.

## 4. INTERNATIONAL ADOPTION IN FINLAND

*Adoption* means constructing a parent-child relation between persons whom with it did not exist before. By Finnish law adoption is a permanent agreement. Adoption is an ancient institution that has existed even before all the laws did. The meaning has nevertheless always been the same: someone who is not capable to have a child takes responsibility of raising someone else's child. First adoption laws were ruled in Western countries during 1920's. (Kats & Krank 1989: 145, 149.) In this chapter I present the history of international adoption in Finland in order to show that there are more parents every year who live with children from different ethnic background than their own, which creates the question of the special skills they need in parenting, something that researchers should take closer look into.

International adoption does not have very long history in Finland - at least the way that Finnish parent's are adopting children from abroad. Actually during 1950's and 1960's Finnish children were given to adoption for foreign couples. Most of the couples came from the United States, Canada, Sweden and Denmark. Foreign parents wanted to adopt Finnish children for example by putting advertisement to a newspaper. Growing amount of childless Finnish couples and the decision to change the Finnish adoption law, however, practically ended Finland's history as a "child giving country" in 1980's. (Kats & Krank: 147-148.) As the volume of domestic adoptions in Finland first started to grow, it quickly decreased year by year so that in the middle 1970's the amount of domestically adopted children was already under 200 in a year. (Parviainen 2003: 30.) Kauppi & Rautanen (1997 cited in Parviainen 2003: 10) state that the reasons for reduction of Finnish children placed to adoption were following: 1) the abortion law from 1970 that decreased the birth-rate of undesired children 2) the laws of day care (from year 1973) and supporting child, and paternity in year 1977 enhanced single mothers economical possibilities to raise their children.

In the year 2000 only 29 children were placed to domestic adoption whereas about 200 children came to Finland by international adoption. (Parviainen 2003: 30.) The amount of new internationally adopted children was the same than the amount of international adoptees reaching the age of adulthood in the late 1990's. That means that the amount of international adoptions was regularized. (Kartovaara 2000 cited in Parviainen 2003: 35.) Parviainen (2003: 35) states that in the light of statistics international adoptions have replaced the domestic adoptions. This means that the amount of domestic adoptions in the 1970's was very close to the amount of international adoptions in the late 1990's. Tilastokeskus (2006) reports that during year 2005 338 children who were born abroad were adopted to Finland. It is 26 children more than in year 2004. Total amount of adopted persons born in either Finland or abroad was 515 in year 2005. That is 14 persons more than in year before. 343 of these adoptees were under five years old. The Table 3 demonstrates the growth of international adoptions in Finland during the last ten years. (Tilastokeskus 2006.)

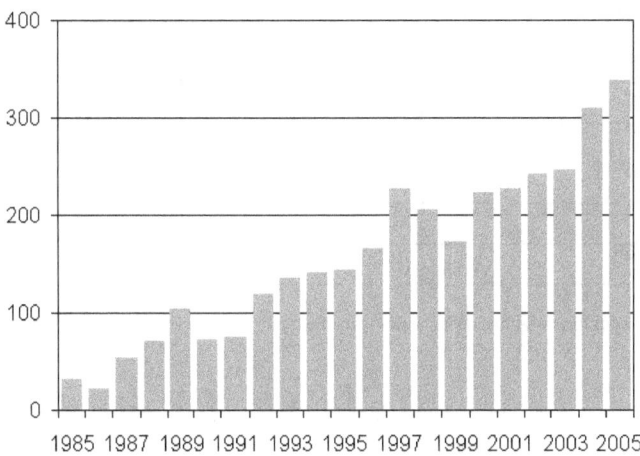

**Table 3. The amount children adopted to Finland during the years 1985-2005 (Tilastokeskus 2006).**

Most of the children that were adopted to Finland in year 2005 came from China (134 children). From Thailand came 59 and from Russia 37 children. These were also the leading countries in the year 2004. (Tilastokeskus 2006.) The statistics covering 10 last years (Table 4) show that most of the children that are internationally adopted to Finland come from these three countries (Adoptioperheet ry, 2006). There is a growth in adoptions of children from totally different ethnic background than their Finnish parents. This means that more and more adoptive parents must develop a certain kind of skills in order to meet their children's unique ethnic and cultural needs (Vonk 2001: 248).

| Country of adoption | The amount of children in years 1985-2005 | Percentage (%) |
|---|---|---|
| Russia | 655 | 23 |
| China | 601 | 21 |
| Thailand | 476 | 16 |
| Colombia | 462 | 16 |
| Ethiopia | 209 | 7 |
| India | 126 | 4 |
| South-Africa | 96 | 3 |
| Estonia | 71 | 2 |
| The Philippines | 49 | 2 |
| Poland | 27 | 1 |
| Other countries | 134 | 5 |
| Total | 2906 | 100 |

Table 4. The countries where from Finnish parents have adopted their children during the years 1985-2005 (Adoptioperheet ry, 2006).

4.1 The International Adoption Process in Finland

Adopting a child internationally or domestically is a long and carefully investigated process. Not everyone can adopt and the potential adoptive parent's have to go through counseling and careful investigations. (Kats & Krank: 149.) The basic guidelines in the law for qualifications for being an adoptive are that: person/parents adopting have to be over 25 years, and still the age gap between the parent and child should not exceed 45 years. If the couple wishes to adopt they have to be married. A single person can adopt but couple just living together without marriage can not. (Laki lapseksiottamisesta 1985.) Different countries have their own different rules for who they would like to give the children to. Nevertheless the qualifications mentioned above are the minimum requirement for people in Finland who wish to adopt, both domestically and internationally, must fulfill.

Adoption does not happen between one day and night; it can take anything from six months to five years, because every adoption process is unique. Table 5 explains the basic process, but every step in it can take different time with different parents. Only the queue to adoption counselling can be one year long in the big cities. The counselling itself lasts about for one year. After that the waiting time for the child information can vary from one to three years. (Adoptioperheet ry, 2006.) This means that the adoptive parents are patient to do all the work to became a parent to an ethnically different child. This information is important when considering my study because it helps to understand the length of the adoption process and, through that, the time that the future adoptive parents have for thinking about how being a parent for international adoptee would be like.

## Adoption process in Finland

```
┌─────────────────────────┐        ┌─────────────────────────┐
│   Attending to          │        │   Travel and            │
│   the adoption counseling│       │   bringing              │
│   in the                │        │   the child home        │
│   social security office│        │   and verifying         │
│   of the home borough   │        │   the adoption          │
│   or in Pelastakaa Lapset ry│    │                         │
└─────────────────────────┘        └─────────────────────────┘
            │                                  ▲
            ▼                                  │
┌─────────────────────────┐        ┌─────────────────────────┐
│   Contact to the        │        │                         │
│   adoption service providers:│   │   Preparations          │
│   The City of Helsinki, │        │   for the travel        │
│   Interpedia,           │        │   new legal papers,     │
│   Pelastakaa Lapset ry  │        │   visas, etc.           │
│   (they provide         │        │                         │
│   information packages  │        │                         │
│   and courses for       │        │                         │
│   future adoptive parents)│      │                         │
└─────────────────────────┘        └─────────────────────────┘
            │                                  ▲
            ▼                                  │
┌─────────────────────────┐        ┌─────────────────────────┐
│   Choosing the          │        │                         │
│   adoption service provider│     │   Getting the information│
│   (different providers  │        │   and accepting the child│
│   have adoption contacts│        │                         │
│   in different countries)│       │                         │
└─────────────────────────┘        └─────────────────────────┘
            │                                  ▲
            ▼                                  │
┌─────────────────────────┐        ┌─────────────────────────┐
│   When the homestudy    │        │                         │
│   is done by the        │        │   Possible              │
│   social security office│        │   progress report       │
│   is ready              │        │   from abroad           │
│   it is sent to the     │        │                         │
│   adoption service provider│     │                         │
└─────────────────────────┘        └─────────────────────────┘
            │                                  ▲
            ▼                                  │
┌─────────────────────────┐        ┌─────────────────────────┐
│   The service provider  │        │   Time to collect,      │
│   applies for           │  ═══▶  │   certify and sent      │
│   the adoption licence  │        │   the legal documents   │
│   from the Finnish      │        │   abroad                │
│   adoption commitee     │        │                         │
└─────────────────────────┘        └─────────────────────────┘
```

**Table 5. The adoption process in Finland. (Helsingin kaupunki, 2006.)**

## 5. DESCRIPTION OF THE RESEARCH PROCESS

I chose to conduct my study by doing a qualitative research because it "is recommend when the goal is to uncover the common and unique experiences of individuals who have first hand knowledge of the phenomenon of interest" (Friedlander et al. 2000: 189). The aim of qualitative research is also to find the point of view of these individuals, and attempt to maintain it through whole research process (Eskola & Suoranta 1998:16). This research is based on ethnographic approach which means describing and analysing the ways people classify meanings. This kind of research never gives complete picture of the whole culture (in this case the culture of Finnish international adoptive parents). The sample represents only part of the reality. Historically this approach was based on observation in anthropological research, but nowadays the data can be collected from events, people or written material. The main interest is not the amount of the interviewees, but the richness of the interview data. (Hautala 2007.) Because the goal of this qualitative study is not to find average connections or statistic regularity (Hirsijärvi et al. 2003: 168), I found the sample of five persons suitable for this case study. The other reason is that these people represent the parents whose children are adopted from three of the top five (see table 4.) adoption countries in Finland (China, Colombia, and Ethiopia). They also represent different geographic locations in Finland (Central Finland, Helsinki Metropolitan Area, and a small town on the coast near Helsinki Metropolitan Area), and both gender (two male and three female).

I collected the research data by conducting half-structured theme interviews. In this kind of method the themes and topic areas of the interviews are defined before hand, but the form and the order, in which the questions are asked, may vary. The format of a theme interview is also so open that an interviewee can speak quite informally, if he/she so wishes. Nevertheless, these themes form a frame work which guarantees that all the interviewees have talked about the same subjects. (Eskola & Suoranta 1998: 87-88.) Interview was the best method for this research, because it gave the opportunity to ask extra questions of certain subject, if needed. (Hirsijärvi et al. 2003: 193.) Interview as a method was also suitable for my research question because the issues I wanted to study were intimate family matters (Metsämuuronen 2001: 40), and because the answers were found, not only by straight questions, but also by "reading between lines" what the interviewees answered to the questions related to the topic.

Of course in every research, that include interviews, there are also some possible problems: the person who is interviewed can feel threaten or scared in the situation, he/she can also act and speak differently than in other informal discussion, because an interview can be a strange situation to him/her, he/she can give the answers that he/she thinks are acceptable or right, even the person would not really think that way, or in this case the person could want to give a good picture of all adoptive parents and children and for that reason avoid talking about problems he/she has faced. (Hirsijärvi et al. 2003: 193.)

5.1 The Aim of the Research and the Research Question

The aim of this study is to understand international adoption in Finland, and what is associated to that phenomenon. I wanted to do that though describing the parents' experiences in international adoptive family, which helps me also to understand what kind of attitudes these parents have taken for being a parent for a child/children from different ethnic background than themselves. The aim of this study is not to create a total picture of all Finnish international adoptive parents, but to look closely to the lives of five families. In order to get better understanding of the challenges of being an international adoptive parent, I discussed about the issues of identity, that highlights the importance of adoptive parents' role in adoptees' identity development, as well as previously presented theories by Vonk and Lee. These chapters form the basis for my research question, which is:

What kind of special skills these international adoptive parents feel they need in international adoptive parenting?

5.2 Conducting the Research

The process of this research begun, when I started to plan it in the early spring of 2006. Later in the spring I wrote the research plan and the literature review. During the summer and early autumn 2006 I read the theoretical literature and similarly started to write the thesis. The interview questions were formed in October 2006 and modulated in December. The tool that I used for structuring the questions for my half-structured theme interviews was Vonk's (2001) recommendations to adoptive parents in the areas of racial awareness, multicultural planning, and survival skills. The questions I used in the interviews were partly based on Vonk's recommendations but I modulated them to be more suitable to Finnish adoptive parents, because I did not want to ask all the things as straight as Vonk's recommendations would have required. An example of this could be the question: are you knowledgeable of and continue to develop respect for the history and culture of your children's ethnic heritage. Instead I asked if the parents have studied their children's birth culture or language, which reveals if they respect their children's roots or not.

I also did not turn the recommendations that Vonk has about ethnic prejudice to straight questions. The reason was that in interview situations people hardly ever answer honestly to a question if they feel that they are or have been somehow racist. So I left out for example the questions: are you able to recognize your own ethnic prejudice, and are you aware of stereotypes and preconceived notions that you may hold toward other ethnic minority groups. I replaced these issues by question: what kind of thoughts you have/have had about the immigrants, which could more easily reveal possible ethnic prejudices or racist attitudes.

I collected the interviewees' explanations of the phenomenon of their special knowledge (the skills they need in living with a child from a different ethnic origin) by interviewing the parents personally. The interviewees were conducted during two weeks: three in the last week of the year 2006 (week 52) and two in the first week of the year 2007 (week 1). Because the interviewees were from the different parts of the country, it would not have been possible to meet all of them face to face. In the name of equality towards all participants, all the interviews were done over telephone. These telephone interviews were audio taped, and I also wrote down notes during every interview. The interviews lasted between 40 minutes to 95 minutes. I aimed to make interview situations confidential and I was also prepared to face possible "locked" situations, which would have been easy for me to solve because the nine years experience from the work as an interviewer (journalist). In these interviewing situations there was, however, no need for problem solving. The atmosphere during the interviews was relaxed, and the whole situation was very conversation-like.

As I used half-structured theme interview (Appendix 1), I had prepared questions that were categorized by themes. The themes I had were: The Family History, About Ethnicity, Skills Needed in International Adoptive Parenting, Supporting the Child's Birth Culture, Issues of Racism, and About the Native Language. I begun all the interviews with same background questions (The Family History), but the questions followed in the order that was natural with a particular interviewee. I went through all the themes and questions with every interviewee, and guided the conversation in the interviews. Even the subjects, which were dealt during the interviews, were intimate family matters, all the interviewees talked in quantity and widely about the themes. The language of the interviews was Finnish, as it was a mother tongue to all the interviewees.

After conducting the interviews, all the material was listened from the tapes and transcribed word by word to a Word document. The analysis was begun by reading through all the interview data, and giving all the interviewees a code (N1-N5). All the interviews were compared to each other by using constant comparison method that includes systematic and intensive study of the research data, sentence by sentence (Metsämuuronen 2001: 26). In this manner the researcher finds indicators (happenings or opinions, etc. in the transcribed texts) which can be combined. The result is that the researcher notices similarities, differences, and in their meanings different levels of similarity. (Metsämuuronen 2001: 25.) Then these indicators were coded according to themes or variables that have arisen from the interview. After time there were categories that were "found to emerge with high frequency mention" and this way became core categories (Dick 2005). These categories were saturated when the interviews did not anymore add new information for the categories (Dick 2005, Metsämuuronen: 26). I have taken advantage of the use of straight quotations when presenting the results of the interview data in this research. Some of the quotations are longer than others, but I have chosen them because they really show the thinking and the argumentation these interviewees went through during the interview. In some cases like for example (N2, see page 52) tells the problems with her teenager Colombian adoptees, it is essential to know the longer story in order to understand why she wonders if it all rises from the genetic and/or cultural background of the children.

As an example of the analysing process, I present here the issue of parents' and children's different ethnic backgrounds. I read through all the transcribed text and marked all the places where parents talked something about ethnic backgrounds. After that I got back to these marked parts of the text and combined them to find if there were similarities and/or differences with the parents. This lead to the formation of the subheading 6.1 called About Different Ethnic Backgrounds. Inside this subheading I still classified the chapters by themes I found that were related to the issue: what the parents thought in the beginning of the adoption process – what weight did the child's ethnic background have in it, what did their friends and relatives think about a child with different ethnic background, parents' opinion about immigrants, and finally how would child's ethnic background affect the way the parents planned to raise the child. I did not give any more subheadings to these classifications in the order that the structure of the research would not look too complicated. The whole transcribed text was analysed and all the chapters (in 6. Results) were formed the similar way that is described here above.

When the data had been classified according to the context, it was compared to Lee's (2003) cultural socialization theory categories that are modified especially to international adoptive families. On account of that I was able to see that Lee's categories were not applicable to Finnish adoptive parents in this study. Because of these findings, I created and named a totally new category that is suitable for these particular Finnish adoptive parents that were researched. Also Vonk's recommendations were modulated to be suitable in Finnish context according to answers of the interviewees.

5.3 Description of the Interview Data

The interviewees were collected by using the snowball sampling. In this method the interviewee recommends other persons he/she considers suitable for the research. It is useful when the sample needed in the research is among the population without clear fixed group. (Le Comte & Preissle 1993: 56–85.) These people were contacted, and when they have given their permission, interviewed, which made the snowball grew. The main demand for the interviewees in this research was that they were parents of an internationally adopted child. There were no qualifications of the child's age or birth country. The parents interviewed to this research were from the area of middle sized city in the Central Finland (three persons) Helsinki Metropolitan Area (one person) and from a small town on coast near Helsinki Metropolitan Area (one person). Two of these international adoptive parents were male and three female. Their children were adopted from China, Ethiopia and Colombia. Because of the delicacy of the research subject, all persons wanted to participate to the research anonym. I have also removed all the information that could help to recognize these persons (name of their place of residence, children's names and exact ages, etc.). I named the interviewees in this study by letter N, number from one to five, and their sex. I present these interviewees here briefly under their codes. All the children were under five years old in the time of adoption, except the Colombian boy who was five and the Ethiopian girl who was six.

*N1* is a mother of an infant girl from China. The family lives in the Helsinki Metropolitan Area. The couple has also teenager girl who has been adopted from Finland.

*N2* is a mother of teenager siblings (boy and girl) from Colombia. The family lives in a small town near Helsinki Metropolitan Area. The couple does not have other children.

*N3* is a father of a toddler girl from China. The family lives in area of middle sized city in the Central Finland. The couple has also two biological children.

*N4* is a father of pre-teenager siblings (boy and girl) from Ethiopia. The family lives in area of middle sized city in the Central Finland. The couple does not have other children.

*N5* is a mother of infant and toddler girls from China. The family lives in area of middle sized city in the Central Finland. The couple does not have other children.

## 6. RESULTS

All the international adoptive parents that were interviewed to this study had travelled a lot in many different countries: many of them because of their own or their spouses' job and the rest of them just for pleasure. This, in some cases, gave also the basis for choosing the country of adoption. Still this decision was most often described to be a mixture of many things: the length of adoption process in different countries that correlated to parents' age, the experience of other adoptive families, the interest/fascination/positive experiences towards/about the culture and the people in some country, some adoptive parents even had friends from or relatives in the country. Only one person revealed that the choice of country "just came from somewhere and there was not any specific reason for choosing the specific country".

It could have been that this international experience that these parents had, could have made them more open-minded and more open to the option of international adoption. This did not, however, come up from their straight answers, but travelling and living abroad were things that all of them emphasized, so it must have effect their worldview and impressions of people from different cultures. All the interviewees are parents of ethnically different looking children, but two of them had first considered adoption from Russia. They did not mention anything about appearance, but people look quite similar to Finns in there. Still the longer length of the adoption process in Russian made them to search other countries, and on the basis of their answers, the choosing of China and Columbia was not hard decision for them to make. It is impossible to say whether these parents would have stayed in the longer "Russia-queue" if they would not have had an experience of the countries they ended up adopting from. The international experience of the adoptive parents is an interesting issue, which could provide good platform for future studies.

(...) varmaan sen takia, et mä oon työn puolesta, tai olinki sillon jo, joutunu matkustaa siellä [Kiina] hyvin paljon, niin tota, niin niin, se varmaan osaltaan vaikutti. Kuitenki se kulttuuri ja maa oli tuttu ja tietysti olin nähny että siellä on lapsia jotka tarvitsi kotia (...) ja prosessi oli hyvin ennakoitavissa (...).
(...)
tiedettiin et Suomesta me ei varmaan toista lasta saada ja sit jossain vaiheessa puhuttiin Venäjästä, mutta tota se jäi aika nopeesti ja koska meillä alko olla siinä adoptoidessa jo ikää, joten me ei haluttu semmosta prosessia mis ei tiedä että kuinka monta vuotta siihen menee ja (...) minkä ikäsen lapsen saa (...). (...) toivottiin, että saatas se mahollisimman pian, että lapsella ois sitte kohtuullisen ikäset

vanhemmat myös mahdollisimman pitkän aikaan. Et osittain se Kiinan nopee käsittelyprosessi oli yks syy kyllä miks siihen ryhdyttiin. Mut toisaalta (...) oli (...) ihastunu siihen kulttuuriin ja ihmisiinki (...).
(N1 Nainen)

(...) probably because, I have because of my work, or had already then, travelled there [China] a lot, so, I think that partly influenced in that. Still the country and culture were familiar, and of course I had seen that there were children who were in a need of a home (...) and the process was well foreseeable (...). (...) we know that we probably would not get another child from Finland, and then in one phase we talked about Russia, but it was left out quite fast, and because we were already getting aged, we did not want that kind of a process in which we would not know how many years it would take and, (...) how old child you will get (...). (...) We hoped that we would get it as soon as possible, and that the child would then have parents who are in reasonable age as long as possible. So party China's fast process was the reason why we engaged in that. But in the other hand (...) we were (...) charmed by culture and people as well. (...)
(N1 Female)

(...) Kolumbia sit sen takia et, valittiin se sen takia, ku siel on oltu. Sitten me ajateltiin, ku me oltii sillo jo yli nelikymppisii, että tota, ne lapset ei oo vauvoja tai ainakaan, että ne on mahdollisesti niiku kouluikäisiä. Ni sitte me tykättiin, että se on sit niinku sopiva maa, ku me kumpiki oltiin sitte opeteltu espanjaa et me voidaan kommunikoida heidän kanssa. Ni sen takia. Venäjä täs nyt ois ollu ehkä helpoin ja Kiina tyttöjen kannalta, mut sit me päädyttiin siihen just tämän takia et me oltiin sen verran iäkkäitä ja osattiin sit espanjaa. Ni siks me valittiin se Kolumbia. (...)
(N2 Nainen)

(...) Colombia because, we chose it because we had been there. Then we thought, because we ere then already over 40 years old, that the children there are not baby, or they are possibly so old that they are already in school. So we thought that it is suitable country, because we both had learned Spanish, so that we could communicate with them. That was the reason. Russia could have possible been the easiest and China when thinking about girls, but then we ended up to this, like mentioned, because we were that aged already and knew Spanish. So that is the reason why we chose Colombia. (...)
(N2 Female)

(...) alussa (...) mulla oli mielessä Intia ja vaimolla oli vissiin Kiina. Ja tota sitten se vaan synty siinä sen prosessin kuluessa. Me oltiin semmosella adoptiovalmennus-kurssilla ja sitten me tavattiin siellä muun muassa semmonen perhe mihkä oli just tullu Etiopiasta sisarukset (...) että toihan on ihan se, se meijän ratkaisu. Se oli sitten aika niinku selvä vissiin kummallekin. Ei siitä sit enää puhuttu. (...)
(N4 Mies)

(...) in the beginning (...) I had India in my mind and wife had China, I think. And then it just was formed during the process. We took part in adoption counselling course, and then we met there, among other people, a family that has just adopted siblings from Ethiopia (...) that is juts our solution! Then it was quite clear for both, I think. We did not talk about it anymore after that. (...)
(N4 Male)

All the parents said that they were getting known the birth culture of their future child before bringing him/her home from abroad. They read books and newspaper articles about the country of adoption, possibly learned the language or some words of the language, and tried to find out "everything that they could" about the birth culture and country. Some also had friends or colleagues from the country, and one person even had relatives living in the country of adoption. One parent had lived in Latin-America, not in the country of adoption that was Colombia, but in a similar culture. Still the information could only split and "one big clod", if the amount of it was too huge.

These results give the impression, that these Finnish adoptive parents really appreciate their children's birth culture, and for that reason want to know everything that is possible about it – possibly in order that they can later tell their children about it as well. It also tells about their personal and genuine interest towards the culture. It is hard to say if it is the character of these parents or the result of the adoption counselling, that makes them to commit so greatly to gaining the knowledge of their children's birth country and culture. In Finland adoption process is also that long that it gives time for preparations and getting familiar with idea of a future child.

(...) Ni oli mulla sitten yks kiinalainen kollega, joka mulle (...) aina (...) kerran viikossa kävi kertomassa kiinalaisesta kulttuurista ja vähän tota erilaisista ruokailutavoista ja tota kielestä ja niin edelleen. Ni ennen sitä ku [lapsen nimi] tuli. Että se oli niinku säännöllinen juttu sitten, että tavattiin ikään kuin kotona yksityisopetusta. Että oltiin itse paperit laitettu jo Kiinaan. (...)
(N1 Nainen)

*(...) Well, I had a Chinese colleague who (...) always (...) once a week visited me and told me about the Chinese culture, and, well, different eating habits and language and so on. It was before [child's name] came. So it was like kind of a regular thing that we met at home, like private lessons. So we had already sent our papers to China. (...)*
*(N1 Female)*

(...) ja ennen ku me mentiin sinne, ni toki mä sitten hirveesti luin. Tai minä etenkin, mut kyllä myös mun mieheni. Luettiin kiinalaisesta kulttuurista ja (...) mitä vähänkin ajankohtasempaa kirjallisuutta, Kiinasta kertovaa, ni luettiin kyllä etukäteen. (...)
(N5 Nainen)

*(...) and before that we went there, I of course read a lot. Or especially me, but also my husband. We read about the Chinese culture and (...) what even little more current literature, telling about China, we read beforehand. (...)*
*(N5 Female)*

(...) kyl se oli aika semmost hajanaista tietoa. Että lähinnä nyt oli vaan koko Afrikka semmonen yks möykky. (...)
(N4 Mies)

*(...) it was that kind of quite scattered information. Above all the whole Africa was just one clod. (...)*
(N4 Male)

## 6.1 About the Different Ethnic Backgrounds

The adoptive parents said that they had paid attention to the fact that their internationally adopted children would look different than themselves and the majority of Finnish population. Two of the interviewed parents told that they did not usually really pay attention to persons' ethnic background, but still it was a thing that was needed to be thought through because of the adoption. One parent told that she thought wider the whole subject of international adoption: its benefits and disadvantages. Every interviewee said that child's different ethnic background was a thing that they paid attention to, in most cases for the sake of the children themselves, because parents were afraid that they would be bullied in Finland because of their ethnic looks.

Typical to these parents was that they discussed with friends and/or relatives about the country of adoption. Still I got the impression that their decision would not have been changed even if someone had been against it. These parents had thought quite deeply what it means to look different, and how the society would react to people who look different than the majority of Finnish population. This reasoning, combined to the gathering information of their children's birth culture, gives the impression that these parents were mentally really well prepared to the international adoptive parenthood.

(...) sillon ihan alussa (...), se Kiina ei ollu vielä kohteena mitenkään selkee, (...) sitä mietittiin, että tietysti sitä, että onko meillä oikeutta ja rasismia ja tämmöstä näin. (...) ja sitten kyl mä mietin niinku sil tavalla, et miten yhteiskunta kokee, tai muut ihmiset kokee kokee lapsen, ja sukulaisilla vähän myös testattiin heidän ajattelua. Emmä tiiä oisko se vaikuttanu mitenkään meijän adoptiopäätökseen, mut tavallaan haluttiin tietää. Mut kyl me sit mietittiin myös sitä, että miltä itestä tuntuu. Et toki yritettiin rehellisesti kaivaa stereotyyppiset kysymykset esille, että miltä itestä tuntuis olla äitinä tai isänä niinku tietyn rotuselle lapselle. Ja yritettiin (...) olla rehellisiä ja sit viel miettiin sitäki, ei niinku ainakaan, jos tuntuu joku niinku kulttuuri tai ulkonäkö sit semmoselta vieraalta, ni ei semmoseen lähetä sitte. Et pitää olla rehellinen jo sen lapsen takia. Me sit tultiin siihen tulokseen tavallaan, että vaikka niinku

ulkomaista taikka kansainvälistä adoptioo voi yhteiskunnan tai niinku makrotasolla kritisoida aika paljon tietysti, et tuodaan tänne vieraaseen kulttuuriin, ni se kuitenki mitä me niinku aatellaa että se mitä me voidaan sille yksilölle tarjota, elikä sille lapselle, et jos se vaihtoehto on kasvaa orpona taikka lastenkodissa esimerkiks Kiinassa tai jossain muussa maassa orpona et me koetaan, et me pystytään tarjoamaan niille paljon enemmän, lasten on parempi olla niinku perheessä.
(N5 Nainen)

*(...) then when we were just in the beginning (...), when China was not yet a clear destination, (...) we thought, of course that, do we have right, and racism and this kind of things. (...) and then I also thought how the community sees it, or how other people take the child, and we also a little bit tested what our relatives thought about it. I do not know if it would have affected to our decision of adoption, but we kind of a wanted to know. But we also thought how we ourselves felt. Of course we tried to honestly dig out the stereotypical questions that how it would feel to be a mother or a father for a child from a certain race. And we tried (...) to be honest and also thought about that, if some culture or appearance feels strange, we would not go for that. So that we have to be honest, even for the child's sake. Then we ended up to the result that, even people can criticize foreign or international adoption quite a lot in the macro level in the community, that you bring [child] here to strange culture, we, however think what we can give to that individual, to that child, if the alternative is to grow up as orphan or in children's home for example in China or in some other country as orphan, so we feel that we can offer them so much more, it is better for the children to be in a family.*
(N 5 Female)

Ei, sil ei oo mitään merkitystä. Mä muistan siinä kotiselvityksessä ja siin adoptioneuvonnassa, ni ne oli meist jotenki semmosii tarpeettomii kysymyksiä. Että ku tää sosiaalityöntekijä kysy, että oletteko tulleet ajatelleeksi, että he ovat tummaihoisia ja ulkomaalaisen näköisiä, kun se ei meille tuntunu taas yhtään miltään. Että me ollaan niin paljon oltu ulkomailla, että me ollaan itte oltu siinä asemassa Sudanissa, et me ollaan ainoot kaks valkosta (...) et meitä tullaan niinku koskettamaan et miltä se valkonen nahka tuntuu. (...) Niissä hakemuskaavakkeissa (...) vielä sai vielä määritellä (...) sillon (...) me sorvattiin siihen (...) niinku eurooppalaisten kaltaisia. Että ku me tiedettiin että siellä [Kolumbiassa] on myös hiilenmustia. Tässä me ajateltiin juuri sitä ettei he nyt niin hirveästi poikkea sit täst [kotikaupungin nimi] väestöstä. Että vaikkei meille itselleen sillä oo mitään merkitystä, mutta heijän kannalta me ajateltiin, et on kivempi et he ei oo ihan hiilenmustia täällä. (...)
(N2 Nainen)

*No, no, it does not mean a thing. I remember when, in this home study and adoption counselling, we thought that these questions were irrelevant. When this social worker asked that have you been thinking that these children have dark skin colour and are foreign-looking, well, we did not think that it was a big issue. We have been so much abroad, and we have ourselves been in the situation in Sudan where we have been the only two white people (...) so that people come to touch us and feel what the white skin is like. (...) In those application forms (...) we still had a possibility to define (...) then (...) we wrote there (...) like, akin to Europeans. Because we knew that there [in Colombia] are people who are dark as the coal. In here we thought just that they would not depart so much from the residents of this [name of the home town]. So even we do not care about that at all, we thought that it would be nicer for them that they are not as black as the coal in here. (...)*
(N2 Female)

Se erinäkösyys tarkottaa tietynlaista ulkopuolisuutta, josta ei pääse eroon eikä sitä pääse karkuun. Mutta se ajatus mikä meillä on, on se kun on sellanen hyvä, vahva lähipiiri, koti, lähiystävät, tuttavat jotka on sellasii joille se ei ole sillä tavalla merkityksellinen asia.
(N3 Mies)

*Looking different means that you are somehow outsider and you can not get rid of that or can not escape it. But the thought we have is, that when you have a good, strong circle of closest people, home, friends close to you, and acquaintances who do not consider that thing so significant.*
(N3 Male)

The friends and relatives have been very supporting through all the interviewees' adoption processes. The adopted children are "the apple of the eye" and no one of the parents received any negative feedback from friends or relatives. The only thing the friends and relatives thought was the same that parents themselves did before adoption: the ethnic background of the children, and the possibility of facing racism.

(....) heidät on vastaanotettu niin sukulaisten kuin naapureiden ja kaikkien taholta niin ihan niinku olis meidän omia lapsia. (…)
(N2 Nainen)

*(…) Relatives, neighbours and everyone has accepted them like they were our own children. (…)*
(N2 Female)

Kenelläkään ei ollu mitään täällä, sellasta niinku yliaatteellista, tätä vastaan. (…) jonki verran oli esillä oli just se, tämä etninen tausta ja erinäkösyys.
(N3 Mies)

*No one in here had anything over-ideological against this. (…) this ethnic background and different appearance were slightly present in conversations.*
(N3 Male)

No, anoppi sano sillo, ku me mietittiin vielä maata, et meillä oli loppusuoralla Etelä-Afrikka ja Kiina, niinku minkä välillä me mietittiin. Ni hän sitte sano, että ottakaa ennemmin Kiinasta. Mä sit kysyin että minkä takia, ni sit se sano, että koska tummaihosta kiusataan enemmän. Et hänellä oli ihan selkeä se, et voihan se olla et pitää paikkansa. Et rasismi on kovempaa afrotaustasilla ja afrikkalaissyntysillä lapsilla sitten. (…) mä sitten kysyin, että miltä susta tuntus ajatus olla isoäitinä lapselle, joka on syntyny muussa maassa. Sitten se sano, et eihän siinä nyt mitään, et laps ku laps. (…)
(N5 Nainen)

36

*Well, mother-in-law said, when we were still thinking about the country, and had South-Africa and China in the final straight, between the ones we were still thinking about. So she said that rather get from China. I then asked that why, and she said that because [children with] dark skin get bullied more. That was clear for her, and maybe it can be true. So that racism is harder for children with afro and African background then. (...) I then ask that how it would feel for you to be a grandmother for a child who has been born in some other country than Finland. Then she said that there is no problem, a child is a child. (...)*
(N5 Female)

Everyone said that they did/do not have any opinion about immigrants before adoption or the opinion was neutral, but then continued their explanation in slightly positive tone. They told that they have followed the conversation about immigrants in Finland from the side, and that it is good to understand different situations in peoples (immigrants) lives. One person described that they, as a couple, are more conscious than average Finnish people about the issues concerning people from different cultures, because they have travelled a lot and had exchange students living in their home. One person analyzed the situation more than the others and admitted that she had some awkward feelings towards the representatives of some cultures.

It is hard to tell if the slightly positive attitude towards immigrants has really been there before adoption or if it has formed later, because the adoption has happened with every parent several years ago. Like the parent with code N2 states: when the own children are "foreigners", it may be that these parents rather want to be neutral when talking about immigrants. It was noticeable that none of the interviewees mentioned the immigrants that would have come from the same birth country as their adopted children. It would be interesting to know if the attitude towards these immigrants would have also been neutral, or would it have been more positive than towards immigrants from more "unknown" countries and cultures? N5's explanation about the countries she could not adopt from proves my interpretation that the experience, and especially positive experience, of certain country probably makes the decision of adopting from there easier. This is interesting also in the means that, it seems that if the parent can not respect the culture, she would not feel able to adopt from there, even the child would be raised in Finland. This is of course only one person's opinion in this case study, but it sounds reasonable in the light of theories presented earlier: if the parent can not support child's identity development by appreciating his or her birth culture, it is difficult for the child to grow up with good self-esteem.

(…) ei ollu mitään voimakasta kannanottoo. Ja nyt varsinkin ku ittellään on ulkomaalaiset lapset, ni en ota voimakkaasti kantaa: niiku, että sanoisin et tänne ei saa tulla yhtään ulkomaalaisia, tai sanoisin et tänne vaan ulkomaalaisia. Että niinkun neutraali, et hyväksyn ulkomaalaiset, mustat ja keltaset ja punaset. (...)
(N2 Nainen)

*(…) did not have any strong attitudes. And especially now when I have got foreign children, I do not have any intense attitudes: like that I would say that I do not want that any foreigners come here, or I would say that come here foreigners. So it is like neutral, I accept foreigners, blacks and yeallows and reads. (…)*
(N2 Female)

No ei mulla mitään sen kummempaa näkemystä tai mielikuvaa, ku tunnen rajallisen määrän maahanmuuttajia ja kaikki ne, jotka tunnen, on oikein mukavia ihmisiä. Et emmä nyt osaa sanoo mitään niistä joita mä en tunne. Et ei mulla semmosta yleistä mielipidettä maahanmuuttajista yleensä tai jostain tietyistä maista tulevista tai kulttuureista tulevista maahanmuuttajista. (…)
(N3 Mies)

*Well, I do not have any particular vision or conception, because I know limited amount of immigrants, and of them that I know are nice. And I can not say anything about them, who I do not know. I do not have any general opinion about immigrants or immigrants coming from a particular country or culture. (…)*
(N3 Male)

Kyl mä luulen, et me ollaan aika suvaitsevaisia. (…) Kyl nyt varmaan rasismia löytyy jos ruvetaan kaivelemaan. (…) Mut emmä nää niinku tämmösiä, et rotu ois niinkään semmonen niinku (…) et jos niitä konflikti tilanteita ehkä tulee jotenki enemmän sitten, kun että on erilaiset tavat niin kulttuurisista syistä. No nyt ku mä rupeen miettimään, ni okei emmä tiiä onko se rasismia vai mitä, mutta (…) mut en varmaan ois esimerkiks islaminuskosesta maasta tuota halunnu adoptoida lasta ittelleni ihan sen takia että, (…) mitä mul on kokemusta siellä maassa olemisesta, ni mun on hirveen vaikee olla naisena islaminuskosessa maassa. (…) Niin mä luulen, etten ois kauheen helpolla lähteny sieltä esimerkiks adoptoimaan, tai semmosesta maasta josta itellään on semmonen kokemus, että ei osaa olla.
(N5 Nainen)

*Yes, I think that we are quite open-minded. (…) Well, I am sure that racism can be found, if we really start to dig on it. (…) But I do not see like, that race would be something like (…) so if there are conflicts, maybe more because of the habits are so different because of cultural reasons. Well, now when I really start to think about it, I do not know if it is racism or what, but (…) probably I would not*

*have, for example, wanted to adopt a child for me from Islamic country, just because of, (...) what are my experiences in being that country, it was very difficult for me as woman to be in Islamic country. (...) So I think that I would have not started adoption process from there very easily, from that kind of a country where I have from the kind of an experience that I really do not know how to be there.*
(N5 Female)

Parents highlighted that they wanted to raise their adopted children by "normal Finnish principles" or by "just living an ordinary life and giving the child a good example". It was also said the children will be Finns. The only thing that segregates them from biological Finnish family is the fact that their adopted child/children look different than the rest of the family. Still they planned to keep signs of their children's birth culture present in everyday life (more in chapter 6.3).

Suomalaisiahan niistä tulee. (...)
(N4 Mies)
*They will become Finns. (..)*
(N4 Male)

(...) me ollaan molemmat suomalaisia ja tota siitä lähtökohdasta me kasvatetaan. Ja kyllä niinku sitäkin mietittiin, että pitää yrittää saada myös se suomalainen identiteetti lapselle kuitenkin aika vahvaks, vaikka siinä rinnalla tulee sitte tää syntymämaa. Et mitä se sitten tarkottaakaan, enkä mä ihan varma oo, et mitä se konkreettisesti tulee tarkottamaan erilaisissa tilanteissa.
(N5 Nainen)
*We are both Finns and from that approach we raise [the child]. And we also thought that we'll have to try to get the for the child quite strong Finnish identity, even there alongside comes this birth country. What ever it means, I am not completely sure what it will mean concretely in different situations.*
(N5 Female)

## 6.2 Special Skills in International Adoptive Parenting

All the parents, that were interviewed, agreed that international adoptive parenting requires some special skills when comparing to biological parenting. Still they did not think that child's ethnic background itself would bring any unique needs for the child, but if there were some, they were thought to be related with medical issues. As the most important skill needed, every parent mentioned the ability to accept how other people will react to a child that comes from different ethnic background. Also the fear of racism and the skills needed in surviving from it, and "tolerance" in general were present. This is not surprising as Finnish people are the nation within European Union that has position as one the nations that is most against the foreigners (Laukkanen 2007). Also the ability to "explain" the children to other people was considered as special skill. One person also mentioned the issues with the way to bond with child who already has an unknown past experiences and other the skills to go trough the adoption process itself.

These results are interesting because they prove that, even the parents highlighted that they want to raise their children as Finns, they are conscious of the reality that being a parent to an ethnically different looking child requires some special skills. This also bundles parents' efforts in learning about their children's culture before adoption. Even the parents did not mention it straight, getting known the culture may have happened, not only for the sake that they could tell their children about their birth culture, but also because it would give them confidence in the situations where they have to explain their child's background to strangers. In the light of these results, the ghost of racism seems to be present in Finnish international adoptive families' everyday life.

No kylhän siinä varmaan just tää, että miten niinku rakennetaan se suhde siihen lapseen. Että sehän on siinä semmonen ehkä kaikkein suurin kysymys. Et ku siel on kuitenki se menneisyys, josta mekään ei tiedetä, eikä hekään tiedä. Se ei oo lähteny se suhde heti siitä syntymästä vaan siin on ollu välissä jotakin.
(N4 Mies)

*Well, there must be this, that, how you bond with the child. That is the biggest question. Because there is anyway the past that we know nothing about, and they do not know either. The bonding has not started straight from the birth, but there has been something in between.*
(N4 Male)

Kylhän siinä ehkä tiettyä semmosta jonkunlaista avarakatseisuutta tarvitaan, että hyväksyy sen lapsen taustan ja ulkonäön ja hyväksyy myös sen jollain tapaa, miten ympäristö reagoi. Must tuntuu, et itellään varmaan eniten minua on just vaivannu se että, (...) lapsi joutus kiusaamisen kohteeks, sen oman erilaisen ulkonäkönsä takia (...).
(N1 Nainen)

*You do need some kind of an open-mindness in accepting the child's background and appearance, and in accepting somehow who the community reacts. I think that I have been most troubled by (...) if the child would be bullied because of her different appearance (...).*
(N1 Female)

Mä en yleensäkään usko, et niinku etnisen tai kulttuurisen taustan kautta tulis mitään erityisiä tarpeita. (...) Varmaan semmonen, mitä kaikki nyt miettii enemmän tai vähemmän, on se et tota etniseltä taustaltaan erinäköset, ulkonäköönhän se yleensä liittyy, ennemmin tai myöhemmin tulevat kuulemaan siitä negatiivisessä sävyssä. (...) et millä tavalla se otetaan sitte vastaan ja millä tavalla sitä käsitellään. Se kai on semmonen mitä pitää pohtia etukäteen jo.
(N3 Mies)

*I do not believe, in general, that ethnic or cultural background would bring up any special needs. (...) Probably one thing that everyone thinks, more or less, is that people with different ethnic background, it is usually connected to the appearance, will sooner or later hear about in negative tone. (...) so how we will take it on, and how we will deal with it. I guess that is a thing that should be thought beforehand.*
(N3 Male)

Kyllä niillä varmaan niitä on [etnisestä taustasta johtuvia erityistarpeita], mutta tota niin ne ei nyt varmaan oo silleen vielä jäsentyny, et lähinnä se tulee siitä erilaisuudesta, että tunnistaa sen oman erilaisuutensa. (...) Erityistaitoja? No kylhän täs joutuu sillä tavalla, jotenki eräällä tavalla, niinku selittämään koko ajan sitä asiaa. Niinku ei sillee biologiset vanhemmat joudu. Tai niinku perustelemaan, selittelemään, perustelemaan.
(N4 Mies)

*I guess they do have [special needs related to ethnic background], but probably they are not structured yet, so it mainly comes from being different, from recognising that they are different. (...) Special skills? Well, in this you have to, in a way, to explain that matter all the time. Like the way biological parents do not have to. Like justify, explain, justify.*
(N4 Male)

Niinku nimenomaan etniseen taustaan, (...) no ei nyt silleen, että tietysti jos miettii niinku sairauksien kohalta tai jotain tämmöstä. (...) He on terveitä kumpikin, että tuleeks sieltä jotain mitä pitäs tietää, (...) et jos on jotain rodulle tyypillisiä kuvioita ni semmost lääkärit ei esim tiiä. (...) No tietysti se prosessi on niiku oma juttunsa, et siihen tarvii [erityistaitoja], ja sen kestää. Mut tärkeempäähän on se (...) et jos rasismia tulee esimerkiks kohalle, et sehän se isoin kysymys on. Pitää jotenki niinku ymmärtää se, et ite ei voi niinku koskaan ymmärtää miltä siitä lapsesta tuntuu. Koska niinku ite ei koskaan koe Suomessa rasismia. (...) Ja sitte jollain tavalla mä luulen, et on hyväksi, et jos on aika semmonen kyky ottaa asioista selvää ja niiku valmis pikkusen vaatimaan erityiskohtelua jos se on tarpeen.
(N5 Nainen)

*Like particularly to ethnic background, (...) well, not really, well, of course if you think about the sicknesses or something. (...) they are both healthy, but if from there comes something that we should know, (...) if there are some sicknesses that are typical for a race, so the doctor [her] would not for example know. (...) Of course the [adoption] process itself is the kind of thing that you need [special skills] to go trough it. But more important is (...) if you face racism, then that is the biggest question. You have to somehow understand, that you can never understand how the child feels. Because you*

*never experience acts of racism towards yourself in Finland. (...) And then I somehow think that it is good, if you have an ability to find out things and are ready demand some special treatment if it is needed.*
(N5 Female)

The adoptive mother, whose teenagers were the oldest of the adopted children at the time of the interview, had noticed problems, and she could not understand if they had arisen because of children's cultural background or for some other reason. This statement rises up a question that I can not answer in this study: how much the genes, and roots in certain culture affect the behaviour of person who has been raised in another culture. It is also noticeable that this boy was five years old in the time of adoption. It may be that like Wickens & Slate stated that children who were placed to their new home and parents in later age, identified more strongly with their ethnicities than those who were placed younger. Virkki (2006) had also similar example from Finland with a girl who was adopted here when she was six years old. She also identified more with her birth culture than Finnish culture, when she was older. This mother's (N2) story does not tell anything about her son's identification, so it is hard to tell where his symptoms arise. The father (N4) of the Ethiopian girl, who was six years old in the time of adoption, did not report similar difficulties.

(...) [lapsuudessa] olen saanu hirveesti heistä ilon aiheita. (...)
No mä oon lukenu, että nytte täs murrosiässä heidän pitäs alkaa niiku kaipailee juuriaan, ja varmaan heil on sellasta. Poika on nyt oikein pahassa murrosiässä (...). (...) Ongelmat alko pojalla jo heti toisella luokalla, ku loppu iltapäiväkerho. Ku hän pääsee kahdelta ja mä tuun neljän viiden maissa kotiin, siin on niiku pari kolme tuntii sellasta, et hän ei oo missään valvonnassa, ni sit hän tekee kaikkee semmost mitä mä hyväksy (...). Ja nyt tyttö on samas vaihees (...) meil on tällästä varastelua, valehtelua, näpistystä, tämmöst niinku jolle ei puhe mitenkään auta. (...) Juuri tää, että selän takana sitten niiku tehdään kaikenlaist jäynää ja koskaan ei myönnetä mitään. Et sitte nyt jotenki ku oikeen neuvotellaan ja tingataan, ni tuumataan, ja hän [tyttö] teki väärin ja pyytää anteeks, mut poika ei koskaan myönnä mitään. Tarviin tähän niiku jotain aikuista apuu, et miten mä jaksan ymmärtää tän, et miks tää menee näin. (...) mitä he viestittää, ni siihen ei mun ymmärrys riitä. Että se niiku tällee vanhalle jäyhälle suomalaiselle, vaik karjalaine oonki, ni on niinku kauheen rankkaa tää tämmönen. Heille se on ehkä luontevampaa tää tämmönen mustavalkoisuus ja tää suunnaton ilo ja sitte tää niinku tämmönen petollisuus. Et ku me nähdään mun miehen kaa näis molemmis sitä samaa, jota hän näki sillon Kolumbiassa ja Ecuadorissa näissä työntekijöissä: että ne on hirveen niinku kivoja, mut sitten todellakin, ni ne saattaa varastaa ja ei koskaan myönnä mitään tai tehdä niinkun rikoksia ja ehdottomasti kieltää kaiken eikä tunnusta mitään. Näis niiku näkyy se samalla lailla. Että kuinka paljon se sit johtuu siitä, että se heidän taustansa törmää tähän suomalaiseen luterilaiseen meininkiin, niin tota kuinka paljon se on sitä ja kuinka paljon se, valitettavasti mä nyt ehkä pikkasen aattelen, mut kuinka paljon se on heidän geneissä. (...) mä oon nyt ymmällä, vanha ihminen, tämän kulttuuritaustan takia, et kuinka paljon siin on sitä että et tää minun systeemini niinku ruokkii sitä, et he toimii näin, ja tai

kuinka paljon sitä, että et se on heissä myötäsyntyistä, se semmonen niinku, ruma sanoo, oman edun tavoittelu.
(N2 Nainen)

*(...) [in their childhood] they brought me lot of joy. (...)*
*Well, I have read that know that they are in puberty age they should start to miss their roots, and probably they do. The boy is now in very bad phase of puberty (...). (...) His problems begin already in the second grade, when afternoon club ended. When he finishes school at to and I will be home around four or five a' clock, there is couple or three hours when he is out of supervising, and he does all kinds of things that I do not accept (...). And the girl is now in the same phase. (...) We have this kind stealing, lying, annexation, and all kinds of this, and talking to them does not help at all. (...) Just this, that they do all kinds of bad things behind my back, and never admit anything. And when we really negotiate and argue she admits that se did wrong, but the boy never admits anything. I kind of a need here some kind of an adults help that I can not understand this, like why is this going this way. (...) what are they trying to communicate, I do not have enough understanding for that. So it is really rough for this kind of an old and austere Finn, even I am from Karelia. This black and whiteness and this enormous joy must be more natural to them, and then this deceitfulness. So I and my husband see in these both the same things that we saw in the employees in Colombia and Ecuador: that they are like really nice, but then they really can steal and never admit anything, and like commit crimes and absolutely deny everything and never confess anything. In these [children] you can this in the same way. Like much it has to whit that their background crashes with Finnish Lutheran lifestyle, so much it is that, or unfortunately I maybe a little bit think, but how much it is in their genes. (...) I am bewildered, old person, because this cultural background, like how much there is that, that this my system boosts that they are behaving this way, or how much that it is in them from the birth this, it is ugly to say but self-seeking.*
(N2 Female)


6.3 Child's Birth Country in Everyday Life

The thing that was typical to all the adoptive parents, was that they did not want to "push" or "overdose" the birth culture to their children. The parents felt and hoped that the birth culture would be a natural thing to their children. Interviewees talked their children about their birth countries' culture in general, eating habits and culture, behaviour in the birth culture, some trivia, and sometimes they talked about news or television programs. One person said that when the child asks something, they answer the questions, but do not otherwise "push" the subject. In one family China was present all the time in everyday life because the parents travelled there regularly.

These answers could be related to the fact about families' aim of Finnish upbringing. It also could be read between the lines that parents wanted that their children would be comfortable with their ethnic roots. It may also be that the parents were afraid that if they pushed their children with the issue too much, they might loose their interest in it.

(...) ettei tarvitse järjestää erikseen mitään Kiina-sessioita, kun se on ihan luonnollista.
(N1 Nainen)
*(...) So we do not have to arrange any special China sessions, when it is totally natural.*
(N1 Female)

Ei olla kerrottu hirveesti, et mitä nyt aina jos lehdest tai tv:stä tulee, tai mitä meil nyt sitte sillon otettu videoo ku heidät haettiin (...). (...) ja sitte joku Shakira, ni tiedetään, että hän on kolumbialainen. (...) jotenki täs arkipäivän elämäs, ni sitä ei kauheesti toitoteta, mut heidän huoneessa on Kolumbian lippu edelleenkin. (...)
(N2 Nainen)
*We have not told [them] that much. When there is something in the newspaper or television, or what we have on the video from the trip when we got them (...). (...) And the like some like Shakira, we know that she Colombian. (...) somehow in this everyday life, we do not really blazon it forth, but in their room they still have got the Colombian flag. (...)*
(N2 Female)

Injeraa, joka on sitte niiden perinneruokaa, ni sitä nyt on joskus [tehty] (...) no sitä nyt pidetään esillä että siel on vähän erilainen ajanlasku, että vuodessa on 13 kuukautta ja uusivuosi on syyskuussa.
(N4 Mies)

*We have sometimes cooked Injera, that is their national food (...) well, that we are trying to have on view that they have got a little bit different calendar there, that they have 13 months in a year and that New Year is in September.*
(N4 Male)

Everyone also revealed that they had books about or from their children's birth country. Also the Finnish adoption books that included a story about international adoption were popular. Parents purchased dolls and toys from the birth country if it only was possible - also if they visited the country, or country alike near it. The interviewees also mentioned that they had in their house ornaments, paintings, furniture (interior decoration), pencil case, clothes, cooking devices, violin with two strings, fairytale CD's and pieces of jewellery. Music was also important, as every parent described that children listen the music from their birth country and some even try to sing it, even they would not know the language or understand the words. Surprisingly many cooked traditional food from their children's birth country. The adoptive parents (3 persons) of Chinese born children told that they celebrate the Chinese New Year and Moon Festival. The families with Colombian and Ethiopian born children did not have any special celebrations. No one included their children's birth cultures traditions to their own traditional celebrations (e.g. Christmas).

Even the parents of Chinese born children were the only ones that celebrate traditional festival from their children's birth countries, it does not necessarily mean that they are more active than the other parents. The Chinese New Year maybe is just the most known foreign feast in Finland. For example in the year 2007 there has been many Chinese New Year happenings in different cities and even the grocery stores have had adverts that mention Chinese New Year. Colombian and Ethiopian feasts are not that known here, and for that reason it could be more difficult to celebrate them. The parents of Colombian and Ethiopian children did not differ from the others in the means of cooking some traditional food and decorating ethnically.

(…) kirjoja on, Kiinasta, kiinaksi, sitten myös suomalaisia, suomeks olevia kirjoja jotka sit kertoo Kiinasta. (…) leluja (…) no suurin osahan niistä on made in China joka tapauksessa. (…) esimerkiks semmonen lasten kartta Kiinasta, että se on tarkotus laittaa kehyksiin seinälle tässä läheisessä tulevaisuudessa.
(N3 Mies)
*(…) we have got books from China, in Chinese, and then we also have got Finnish books that tell about China. (…) toys (…) well, most of the toys are made in China anyway. (…) for example that kind of a children's map from China, that we have planned put it to frames in this near future.*
(N3 Male)

Ja [lapsen nimi] huone on sisustettu kyllä kiinalais-suomalaisittain. (…) mutta, et kyl se niinku, vaikka länsimaalainen huone onki, mut, et siellä on viitteitä sitten hänen etniseen taustaan.
(N1 Nainen)
*And [child's name] room is decorated as Chinese-Finnish-way. (…) but sit it is like, even it is a Western room, it still has references to her ethnic background.*
(N1 Female)

(…) perhejuhlissa ei sit oikeestaan muuta, ku et ainoo mitä on se kiinalainen uusivuosi on, ni kyl me sillon ollaan laitettu joitain koristeita ja käyty syömässä kiinalaisessa tai yritetty jotain kotona tehdä. Aina muuten perhejuhlat vietetään ihan suomalaisen kulttuurin mukasesti. (…)
(N1 Nainen)

*In the family celebrations we do not have anything else but only the Chinese New Year, when it is, we have been put on some decorations and gone to a dinner to Chinese restaurant or have tried to make something at home. All the other family celebrations we spend normally according to Finnish culture.*
(N1 Female)


All the interviewees have participated, or still do, meetings with other adoptive families in general and/or with families who have adopted from the same country as they had. Some of them had also stayed in contact with the group of parents with whom they were bringing the children home from their birth country. Two parents told that it was more than three years ago when their families had participated to some kind of meetings. The most active ones met other adoptive families several times a year. Two persons also had some adult family or other friends from different cultural backgrounds, and one was planning to participate to university's friendship family program some day later.

Adoptive parents did not explain exhaustively their reasons for attending these meetings. It could be that they wanted their children to meet other children who come from the same birth country. Probably the parents also wanted to exchange thoughts about being adoptive parent. Under the surface could also be issues about child's development and behaviour. It must be easier talk about possible problems or other issues with people who had gone through similar things.


(...) on pidetty yhteyttä sekä muihin Kiinasta adoptoineisiin että sitten me ollaan ajateltu tällä tavalla tää (...) pitää niiku yllä sitä, että noita muita Aasiasta tulleita, myös aikuisia meillä niinku tuttavapiirissä. (...) Meil on sellasta niinkun epävirallista, epämuodollista yhteenliittymää (...) joskus kesällä kerääntyy (...) puolen tusinaa perhettä yhden perheen kesäpaikkaan, (...). muutenkin tietysti Kiinasta adoptoineiden perheiden kanssa (...) hankkiuduttu tutuiksi.
(N3 Mies)

*We have stayed in contact with other [families] who have adopted from China, and then we have thought this way that we like need to keep on that we have those other people who have came from Asia also as our acquaintances as adult age. (...) We have that kind of a, like unofficial get-together thing (...) sometimes in the summertime half dozen of families get together in one families summerhouse, (...). And also we have got known (...) other families who have adopted from China.*
(N3 Male)


(...) meil on kuitenki semmonen kulttuuriryhmä, mihin nää perheet, jotka on adoptoinu Etiopiasta, ni pari, kolme kertaa vuodessa tapaa toisiansa ja pitää sitten yhteyttä. Säännöllisesti ja epäsäännöllisesti.

(...) kyllähän nyt sitten tapaa, tota niin noissa adoptioperheiden tapaamisissa muista maista myöskin.
(N4 Mies)

*(...) we have, however, that kind of a culture group, where these families that have adopted from Ethiopia meet each other couple-three times a year, and stay in contact. Regularly and irregularly. (...) of course we meet people from other countries in those meetings for adoptive families.*
(N4 Male)

6.4 About the Identity

All the interviewees stated that they feel that it is important to support their child's identity building. They listed many ways of doing it. One that everyone mentioned was: reading books about adoption (most of them fairytales) to the children. Parents also urged upon their children that people are different (not only in the means of adoption or skin colour but also in the means of talent, etc.) and that is the fact everyone should respect. The interviewees also tried to explain their children the reasons why they became adopted.

The parents did not explain why supporting the identity is an important thing for them. They either questioned that they should be doing so. Again I would look to the Finnish adoption counselling that may have a role in parents understanding of identity issues. It can also be so that these parents have been getting known this kind of literature, but just did not bring it up in the interviews.

(...) et ne sit jatkossa ymmärtäis, et joskus olosuhteet on vaan semmoset, että ihmiset joutuu tekee valintoja. Ja, ja toisaalta ni, et ne on olleet hyvin haluttuja, et me ollaan heitä toivottu koko ajan. Et vaikka biologiset vanhemmat on joutunu jättämään ni, oli se tapa ollu sitte mikä tahansa, ni olosuhteet aina sit vaikuttaa (...).
(N1 Nainen)

*(...) so that they would understand in the future that the circumstances just are that kind of that people have to make choices. And in the other hand, that they have been really wanted, and we have hoped for them all the time. Like even the biological parents must have left them, what ever the way has been, the circumstances always affect on that (...).*
(N1 Female)

Parents have also other ways of supporting their children's identity. They told them how beautiful their skin colour is, how wonderful their roots are and how proud the parents are of them, and also without words: showing the appreciation in everyday life.

(...) niinku kehutaan ja ylistetään sitä, et he on kolumbialaisia. Et miten se on hienoo, et tänne härmäläisten junttien joukkoon tulee vähän tälläst väriä.
(N2 Nainen)

*(...) like we boost and praise the fact that they are Colombian. That how great it is, that we can have this kind of colour among these hillbillies from Härmä.*
(N2 Female)

(...) myöskin sitä kautta, että kun me ollaan tavallaan, niinku arvostetaan kiinalaista kulttuuria, ja mitä niinku kiinalaises kulttuuris on saatu aikaan. (...) Et mä en usko semmoseen, et myytäs jollain tavalla sitä, selitettäs kuinka hienoa se on. Että kun se on meidän elämässä just, musiikki, taide, ruoka, jonkun verran historiaa ja näin ni, siinä niinku lähtee siitä meidän normaalista elämästä. Sitä kautta se tulee se arvostuskin. Eihän se olis meijän elämässä jos ei olis sillai tavalla niinku, hyvää ja arvokasta.
(N3 Mies)

*(...) also that way, that we are in a way, that we like appreciate Chinese culture the achievements in Chinese culture. (...) Like I do not believe in that we would sell it somehow, like we would explain how great is. Like when it is in your lives now the music, the art, the food, a little peace of history, and so on, it like comes from our normal life. Trough that comes the appreciation. It would not be in our lives, if it would not be, like, good and valuable.*
(N3 Male)


(...) me yritetään (...) et siihen ei sisältys mitään itsenäistä ja mystistä ja kummallista siihen niinku kiinalaisuuteen. Et sitten sitä, adoptiotausta on niinku oma juttunsa, ja jotenki niinku yritetään siihen, että kiinalaisuus pysys tämmösenä hyvänä juttuna ja toivon mukaan voidaan matkustaa siellä joitakin kertoja (...). (...)
(N5 Nainen)

*(...) we try that (...) there would not be anything independent mystic, like, in being Chinese. And then this adoption background is like separate thing, and somehow, we like try, that being Chinese would stay as a good thing, and we try to travel there few times (...). (...)*
(N5 Female)


The parents told that the small children asked very little or not at all about their background. Of course the youngest children were only two years old, so they do not really completely understand the concept of the adoption yet. The older children were little more interested about their birth parents. Still, what ever the age of the children, all the parents said that they expect the questions to rise "later". The children seemed to be, however, also interested about the trivia of their birth country, and had even "funny" questions.

The fact that all the interviewed parents have presented their children's birth culture openly in everyday life may have been one reason why the children did not feel so much need to ask about subject deeper. The parents' message seemed to be that, whatever the questions, they tried to find an answer to it and keep the atmosphere open. Probably they trusted that if there is not anything "hidden" in their children's background, it would help them in healthy identity development.

(...) paljonko kiinalaiset saivat palkkaa kun rakensivat Kiinan muurin? Et ihan niinku mitä tulee eteen, niinku silleen, et erilaisia asioita. (...)
(N5 Nainen)
*(...) how much the Chinese got paid when they built the Great Wall of China? Like what ever they can come up with, like different things. (...)*
(N5 Female)

(...) jotain on ollu niinku ruokailusta ja niinku syömäpuikoista (...). Jotain miten sanotaan sitä ja tätä kiinaksi ja ihan tämmösii asioita, et ei se vielä pohdi mitenkään kauheen syvällisesti sitä, et minkälaista se elämä siellä sitte on ja muuta mutta tota. Ei se myöskään oo kyselly miksi hänet oli jätetty (...).
(N1 Nainen)
*(...) there has been something about eating, and like chopsticks (...). Like how you say this and that in Chinese, like these kind of things, she does not philosophize what kind of life it has been living there and else. And it has not been asking why it has been left (...).*
(N1 Female)

(...) [poika oli adoption aikaan] täyttänyt viisi. Hän muistaa siit sijaisperheestä ja hän muistaa oman äitinsä ja muistaa viimesimmän isänsä. Ja joitakin kertomuksia, että hänellä on semmosta, just sellasii järkyttävii muistoja, joita hän kerto espanjaks ja joskus hän sit puhelee, on puhellu niist suomeks. Ja tota sit tyttö taas kyselee sillä lailla, että hän on kuullu, että poika on puhunu. (...) Että ja on nyt ihan tänä vuonna puhetta ollu siitä, että ei tiedetä että onko teidän biologinen äiti elossa vai ei, että kun näin on käyny, että hän on hävinnyt. Et meillä papereissa lukee, että äiti on niiku kadulla. Et äiti on heidät jättäny ja poika muistaa että naapurin setä piti heitä, ja ku äiti ei tullu takasin (...). (...)
(N2 Nainen)
*(...) the boy had turned five [during the adoption]. He remembers about the foster family, and remembers his own mother and his latest father. And some stories he has got, that kind of shocking memories, that he told in Spanish, and sometimes he talks, have been talked about them in Finnish. And well, the girl then asks the way that she have heard that the boy has talked. (...) And now during this year we have talk about the fact that we do not know if your biological mother is alive or not, because it has been the way that she has disappeared. That in our papers it says that mother is like on the street. Like mother has left them, and the boy remembers that the man next door kept them when mother did not come back (...). (...)*
(N2 Female)

(...) ku meillä nyt on näitä tuttuja, joilla on sitten näitä Kiinasta adoptoituja lapsia, eri ikäsiä. (...) Ni vähän niinku sitä kautta tietysti on hahmottunu sekin, että minkälaisia kysymyksiä sieltä niinku jossakin vaiheessa ehkä saattaa tulla.
(N3 Mies)
(...) now that we have these acquaintances who have adopted children from China, in different ages. (...) So though that we have got a hint of what kind of questions there can be arising.
(N3 Male)

(...) no lähinnä ne kyselee niihin omiin vanhempiinsa liittyen kysymyksiä, ja niinku siihen perheeseen. Ku siit on hirveen vähän, meinaan tietoa. Ni tota, niitä ne varmaan sitten fantasioi, niihin liittyviää asioita.
(N4 Mies)
(...) well, mostly they ask questions related to their own parents, and like the family. And we have so less information about that. Well, they probably fantasise things related to these.
(N4 Male)

(...) tietysti sitä on, et adoptiotaustaan liittyy, ni kiinnostavaa oli joskus keskustelu siitä et kaikki kiinalaiset lapset joita me tunnetaan ni on adoptiolapsia, ni [lapsen nimi] ihmetteli sitä, et onks Kiinassa aina sillä tavalla, et lapset adoptoidaan. Jollonka mä jouduin tietysti selittämään, et ei, et kyllä se on ihan, suurin osa kyllä elää niissä biologisissa perheissään, erisanoin selitin, että kuitenkin. Mut kyl se niinku, kaikenlaisia kysymyksiä tulee, niinku kaikkee mahollista, miks kiinalaisilla on musta tukka ja tällästä. Me ollaan yritetty selittää, et Kiina on iso maa ja silleen.
(N5 Nainen)

(...) what has to with the adoption background is the conversation we had about that all the Chinese children we know are adoptive children, so [child's name] wondered that it is always that way that in Chine children get adopted. When I of courses needed to explain that, no, that majority of them do live in their own biological families, well I explained it in different words, but still. But is it like, all kinds of questions arise, like everything that is possible, why Chinese people have black hair and that kind of things. We have tried to explain that China is a big country and like that.
(N5 Female)

Two parents told that their children had given some symptoms that they would like to look more like their parents and friends. Even the three other parents did not have similar experiences, they told that they also give positive feedback about their children's appearance.

Because the looks reveal the absence of the biological tie between ethnically different looking parents and children, the appearance is something that is discussed in every family. The parents have chosen to praise to their children's looks, possibly as a counterbalance against the comments their children have heard or could be hearing from strangers. It can be read between the lines that the parents think that if their children appreciate their looks themselves, it is a good defence against nasty or racist comments. The interviews can be also interpreted the way that the parents want their children to think that instead of looking different they should feel that they look unique and they have that kind of a beauty that ethnically Finnish people can not achieve.

(...) no kyllä se on joskus saattanu sanoo, että äiti sitte, ku mä oon iso, ni mulle tulee samanlainen tukka ku sulle (...). Mut ei se ole niinku harmitellu kuitenkaan, että onpas mulla väärän väriset hiukset tai jotain muuta. Mut kyl se tämmösessä, jos se on sitte ilmenny, että tulevaisuuden odotuksissa, että et hän on sitte enemmän näkönen (...). (...) se [vastaaminen lapsen sanoihin] on kai menny vähän leikin puolelle, että tota, hän kuitenkin ymmärtää, että hänellä on hienon väriset hiukset ja kauniit silmät, ja muuta, että voi että ku ois itellä samanlaiset.
(N1 Nainen)
*(...) well, it could have sometimes said that mother when I am big I will have same kind of hair as you do (...). But it has not anyway pitied that I have wrong coloured hair or else. But if it has become apparent, it has been in these kind of future expectations, that she will look alike more (...). (...) the [answering to child's questions] has been a bit joking, that she anyway understands that she has got a great hair colour and beautifully coloured eyes, and else, I wish that I had the same.*
(N1 Female)

(...) ku heil on ihanat mustat tukat, ni aina sitte, ku mul on vaalee ohut, ni mä aina sitte, et miten ihanat hiukset, voi miten ihana kiilto. He mielissään kuuntelee sitte, he ei koskaan niiku sano, et he haluis valkoset. (...) et sitä aina, et miten teil on kaunis ihonväri. Et tota he ei missää nimes niinku, en usko, et ei ainakaa näy päältä, et he pitäis itseään niiku mustina tai rumina.
(N2 Nainen)
*(...) because they have lovely black hair, and then always, that I have got thin and blond, so I always, that how lovely hair and what a wonderful shine. They listen that and are pleased, and never say that they would like to have white. (...) like that always, that how you have got lovely skin tone. So they do not in any case, at least I do not believe, you can not see from the top, that they would consider themselves as black or ugly.*
(N2 Female)

(...) esimerkiks [lapsen nimi] haluis, et se sais oikastua noi hiuksensa, ku sil on kauheen kikkarat hiukset. Mut sit toisaalta se saa semmosta viestiä muilta että ku ne ihailee sitä, et ku sul on niin hyvät hiukset tai hienot hiukset ni. (...) kyl me on koitettu vähän niiku rohkasta siinä, että ole ylpeä vaan siitä mitä sulla on itellä.
(N4 Mies)

*(...) for example [child's name] would like to straighten her hair, because she has got so curly hair. But in the other hand she receives a message from others that they admire that you have so nice or great hear. (...) yes, we have tried to courage her a little bit that be proud of what you have got.*
(N4 Male)

These adoptive parents had learned at least some words of their children's birth country's language. Some children had also already learned the language, but all of them forgot it in about six months after arriving to Finland. None of the children is studying the language at the moment, and all the parents wait if they later on would like to do so. At the moment the lack of time was the biggest reason why the children did not study the language of their birth country. However, trip to the birth country was in the plans, or had at least been in the thoughts of almost all of the families. Like with deeper telling about their children's background, the parents also seemed to wait their children's own interest with the language studies. Could that interest rise in future from the trip to children's roots?

(...) mut että sehän vaatis ihan, kielenoppiminen, semmosta jatkuvaa altistusta silleen. Ja sitä me ei nyt oo tän ajan puutteen vuoksi jotenki pystytty järjestämään. Että varmaan tästä pääkaupunkiseudulta sais jonku, joka kävis sit kotona koko ajan, mutta ei oo nyt sellast tullu järjestettyä. Että mä kyllä haaveilen siitä, et jonain päivänä me voitas käydä yhdessä vaikka kiinan kielen kurssilla.
(N1 Nainen)
*(...) but it would demand just, learning the language, that kind of, being exposed to it continually. And, because of this lack of time, we could not have been able to arrange it. That probably from this Helsinki Metropolitan Area we could find someone who would visit our home all the time, but we just have not happened to arrange that. I am dreaming about that one day we could participate together, for example, Chinese class.*
(N1 Female)

(...) mehän suunnitellaan Kiinan-matkaa. Ne on kauheen kiinnostuneita siitä, haluais lähteä molemmat lastenkodissa vierailemaan ja silleen. Et se on musta semmonen peruspositiivinen vire, on et, mikä on kiinalaista ni on kiinnostavaa. (N5 Nainen)
*(...) and we are planning a trip to China. They are extremely interested in it, they would both like to go and visit the children's home, and so on. Like, I think it is a positive vibe, like that, what is Chinese is interesting.*
(N5 Female)

(...) se on sitten vähän niinku omasta kiinnostuksesta sitten kiinni. Että ei me nyt ruveta niiku tavallaan pienenä lapsena laittamaan mihinkään Kiinakouluun. (...) totta kai, menköön opiskelemaan kiinaa, jos haluaa, mutta ku umpisuomenkielinen on, ni vaikeeta se voi olla.
(N3 Mies)

*(...) it will depend on the own interests then. That we will not start to, kind of a, as a small child to put her into a China school. (...) of course, [she can] go study China, if she wants, but it can be difficult, as she is completely Finn.*
(N3 Male)

(...) tällä hetkellä ei oo mahollisuutta, tai tuntuu, et sitä kotona olo aikaa tarvitaan ni, (...) lähtee kehittämään jotaki, et ois kerran viikossa joku Kiinakerho tai joku semmonen, mut että ajan kanssa sit myöhemmin. Ja kyllä mä oon [lapsen nimi] kanssa varsinki jutellu siitä, että haluisko se joskus opetella kiinaa, ni tässä vaiheessa se sanoo, et joo (...). Mut täytyy nyt kattoo, et mikä se tilanne sitte on ku on ikää vähän enemmän. (...) Mut kyl me koko ajan puhutaan, tai niinku aika toistuvasti puhutaan, näistä asioista, et jos sitten haluaa, ni pyritään ettimään se tapa, jolla sen voi toteuttaa.
(N5 Nainen)

*(...) we do not have any possibility at the moment, or that it feels that we need the time home (...) so to start develop something that once a week would be a China club or something like that, but maybe later, with time. And yes, I have been especially talking with [child's name] that would she like to learn Chinese some day, and in this phase she says yes (...). But let's see what the situation is when she is little bit older. (...) But we do talk all the time, or like quite continuously, about these things, that if she then wants something, we start to search the way that she can accomplish it.*
(N5 Female)

6.5 Issues of Racism

Facing strangers who ask questions about adopted children is almost daily for all the international adoptive parents in this study. They described that meeting these people and their questions was quite ok when the children were so young that they did not understand anything. But when the children grew older, parents started to find these questions more and more prying and impolite.

Ability to handle these kinds of situations was one of the skills that the parents considered important in international adoptive parenting. And here is also present the theme of looking different, which has been present during this whole study. It is a fact that can not been changed, and it is always noticed. Every adoptive parent must develop their own "surviving" system in the situations like these.

(...) jotenki se oma suhtautuminen vähän muuttuu, ku lapsi alkaa ymmärtää, että hänestä kysellään. Ja kiusalliseks mä oon kokenu nimenomaan sellasen, et (...) kaupan kassa kysyy, että onko he sisaruksia, jolloinka minulle se on sillain, että ei se heille kuulu. Mä sit vaan vastaan, että on he sisaruksia, että he on molemmat meijän lapsia. Et ne itseasiassa haluu nyt tietää, että onko he biologisia sisaruksia. Mut että (...) siinä niinku kyseenalaistetaan sitä heidän sisaruussuhdettaan. Ni (...) ei kaupan kassan tarvii

semmosta kysellä. (…) Siitä ollaan ihan miehen kanssa puhuttukin, että pitää niinku omalla esimerkillä yritttää, niinku että sitten vastaa siihen että jos kysytään meiltä tämmöstä (…) että totta kai he on.
(N5 Nainen)

*(…) the own reaction somehow changes when the child's starts to understand the people make questions about the child. And I have felt irritated especially (…) when the cashier asks if they are siblings, when I feel that it is not their business. Then I just answer that they are siblings, they are both our children. What they really want to know is that if they are biological siblings. But that (…) in that it questions their sisterhood. So (…) the cashier does not need to make that kind of questions. (…) We have even talked about that with my husband, and we have to try with our own example, like if someone asks something like that [we answer] (…) that of course they are.*
(N5 Female)


Ulkopuoliset kyselee ja kiinnittää huomiota hänen hiuksiinsa ja silmiinsä. (…) Totta kai sit tulee selitettyä ehkä näitä [lapsen nimi] taustoja ja just sitä, että mistäpäin maailmaa hän on ja muuta (…).
(…)
(N1 Nainen)

*Strangers ask questions and pay attention to her hair and eyes. (…) Of course you end up explaining these [child's name] backgrounds and just that from where she is from and else (…). (…).*
(N1 Female)


(…) tota miten sen nyt sanois. Tietysti omat lapset on aina tosi sulosia, mutta tää on nyt silleen aivan poikkeuksellisen sulonen. Et siin on välillä (…) esimerkiks oltiin tämmösessä isommassa juhlatilaisuudessa ja tota vaimo oli mukana ja sitte lapset oli mukana, kaikki kolme. Ja siinä sitten semmonen rouvashenkilö kävi kovasti ja vuolaasti kehumassa kuinka sulonen tämä nuorimmainen on. Ja nämä kaks vanhempaa lasta seiso siinä vieressä. Että semmosetkaan tilanteet ei oo kauheen mukavia näitten vanhempien lasten puolesta. Ei ne ite sitä sillai välttämättä kokenu, että ne on tietysti ylpeitä pikkusiskostaan, mutta tota siinä tavallaan ei ite viitti sanoo sille ihmiselle [joka sanoo], että (…) ei noin sulosia lapsia muita olekaan ni, sanoo että jotain semmosta "paitsi että nämä kaks muuta tässä". Että ku se on sit sillai, et mä en halua semmosta niiku eriarvosuutta eikä meijän perheen sisällä semmosta oo, eikä tuttavapiirin kanssa oo mitään. Et meijän lapset on meijän lapsia, kaikki kolme ihan samalla tavalla.
(N3 Mies)

*(…) and, well, how I would put it. Of course the own children are always cute, but this one is like particularly cute. That you are sometimes like (…) for example when we took part in this kind of bigger festive occasion, and I had my wife with me, and my children with me, all three. And then one lady came and told swiftly how cute this youngest one is. And these two older children were standing straight next to it. Like those kinds of situations are not really nice either, when thinking about these older children. They probably did not feel it like that themselves, they are of course proud of their sister, but in a way you do not dare to say to that person [who says] that (…) there is no other such cute children, so say something like "except these two other here". That, because it is like, I do not want to have like inequality, and we do not have that in our family or with the circle of acquaintances. Like our children are our children, all three in same ways.*
(N3 Male)

If the questions were adjusted straight to the child, they knew how to answer to them, even the parents told that they had not really "taught" them to do so. This may reflect the naturalness of adoption, open atmosphere and good identity development the parents talked about: there is nothing to be ashamed of in being adopted.

Kyllä mun sydäntä lämmitti suuresti semmonen, kun tavattiin yks tuttava jota ei oo useisiin vuosiin nähty, eikä hän tota tienny että meillä on kolmas lapsi, saatikka että kolmas lapsi ois adoptoitu. Ja hän siinä sitten tokas että "mistäs tämmönen tyttö on tullu?", niin tämä kaksvuotias vastaa että "isä ja äiti haki Kiinasta". (...) Tää on niinku sen tyyppinen suhde minkä minä toivon adoption siis olevan. Se on semmonen luonnollinen ja normaali osa elämää, että mä oletan, et jos kaksvuotiaalla on tämmönen suhde siihen asiaan, mikskä se siitä sitten kauheesti muuttuu. Totta kai se problematisoituuu enemmän tai vähemmän sitten myöhemmin, mutta se on semmonen asia mihin suhtaudutaan avoimesti ja normaalisti.
(N3 Mies)

*It really warmed my heart greatly, when we met one acquaintance we had not seen in many years, and that person did not know that we had a third child, let alone that the third child would be adopted. And this person there blurted out that "from where has this kind of came?", and this two-year-old answers that "father and mother got from China". (...) This is like that kind of an attitude that I wish adoption would be. It is that kind of normal and natural part of life, and I expect that if two-year-old has this kind of an attitude to the thing, how it would then so much change. Of course it becomes more or less problematical then later, but it is thing that we adopt an open and normal attitude to.*
(N3 Male)

(...) että ei meillä oo mitään semmosta, miten mä nyt sanosin, jotain semmosta "täsmäkoulutusohjelmaa" ollu, että jos sulta joku kysyy ni vastaat näin ja näin. Et sitä mukaan, ku niit tilanteita on tullu (...). (...) Ni sit on niistä jotenki selvitty. ja niistä keskustellaan, mut hyvin silleen kevyesti kuitenki.
(N1 Nainen)

*(...) that we do not have anything like, how I would say it, something like "specific training program" that is someone asks you, you answer like this and this. Like as those situations have come (...). (...) We have somehow managed them, and we discuss about the, but still very lightly.*
(N1 Female)

All the parents had given a thought for their place of residence. Still no one considered moving somewhere else, even thought one parent pondered that Helsinki Metropolitan Area could have been also a good place to live because its multiculturalism. Working places and already bought houses also affected the decision to keep living in the same as before adoption.

No, kyl me nyt mietittiin sitä, mut ei nyt sillä tavalla, et me mihinkään oltas oltu muuttamassa. Lähinnä niinkun sellasella teoreettisella tasolla että, että vois olla helpompaa asua pääkaupunkiseudulla, koska se on monikulttuurisempi kaiken kaikkiaan. Mut tietysti sekään ei oo niinku, kaikkial on omia ilmiöitään.
(N3 Mies)

*Well, we thought about it, but not that way that we would have been moving anywhere. Mainly like that kind of a theoretic level that it could be easier to live in Helsinki Metropolitan Area, because it is overall more multicultural. But of course that is not either like, everywhere is different and own phenomena.*
(N3 Male)

(…) no, ei me nyt varmaan mietitty sitä sillä tavalla, että me oltas lähdetty niinkun vaihtamaan asuinpaikkaa sen takia. Oli tämä talo ostettu silloin 10 vuotta sitten ja oli sillon joku neljä ja puoli vuotta tässä asuttu. (…)
(N4 Mies)

*(…) well, probably we did not think it the way that we would have changed our place of residence because of that. We had bought that house 10 years ago, and during that time we had lived here four and half years. (…)*
(N4 Male)

Facing racism was not a familiar experience for the parents with small children. The older children, how ever, had faced some bullying in school or hobbies, but parents interfered in these situations and they were solved. Parents also told that they have given their children advice how to handle those kinds of situations. Smaller children did not yet have had experiences of bullying in the day care. Still the parents had already started to plan how to discuss about the issue if the time comes later. The experiences of the parents of the older children prove, that adoptive parents' fear of racism in not groundless. They feel helpless because they can not themselves protect their children from racism.

Poika on kova urheilemaan, ja tota näissä otteluissa ni vitun katuneekeriks nimitellään ja näin. Et kyllähän siihen on törmänneet. Ja sitten kotona on niiku just sanottu, että ku nyt siit neekerist on tullu haukkumanimi, et nytte niinku paras konsti on se, että ei niiku noteeraa tai korkeintaan sanoo et valitettavasti en oo aito, oon vaan sekundaa. Mut sitte ku on siinä tilanteessä ni hän tekee just silleen ku heistä tuntuu, että enhän mä voi siihen vaikuttaa. (…)
(N2 Nainen)

*The boy used to go in for sports a lot, and in this match's he was being called fucking street nigger, and so. So they have bumped into that. And then at home we have said that, now when that nigger has become a term of abuse, so now the best way is to be like you would not notice at all, or at most say that unfortunately I am not genuine, I am just second-rate. But when he is in that situation, he does just the way he feels, and I can not influence on that. (...)*
(N2 Female)


(...) [lapsen nimi] ei varmaan negatiivisia kokemuksia siitä kauheesti ihan. No yks ainoo, joka hänelle ei muistu mieleen, (...) se oli mun miehen siskon luona hoidossa, ja kerran ku ne oli ollu kaupungilla kävelemässä, ni joku vanhempi nainen oli tullu ja sylkässy päälle. Ja mitäs se oli nyt sanonu, jotai kuitenki et "tommosia täällä tarvita", tai jotain niiku. Mut, et se oli enemmä ollu niinku ilmeisesti kohdistettu tähän mun mieheni siskoon, et ku se oli arvellu että hän ois tehny lapsen jonku ulkomaalaisen kanssa tai muuta että. (...) Mut se on ainoo kerta, ku on ollu semmosta niinku ikävää palautetta, et kyllä siihen pieniki lapsi sit joutuu siihen joskus osalliseks tälläseen. Et en tiedä sit muuta, mut nyt esimerkiks ku hän on ollu päiväkodissa elokuusta lähtien, ni hän on tosi hyvin siellä ryhmän jäsenenä.
(N1 Nainen)

*(...) [child's name] does not probably have so many negative experiences. Well, one and only that she can not recall, (...) it was in the care of my husbands sister, and once they were having a walk in the city, some older woman came and split on her. And what has she said, anyway something like "we do not needed that sorts of in here", or something like that. But apparently it was more aimed to my husbands' sister, because it has considered that she had had a baby with a foreigner, or something. (...) But it is the only time when there has been some kind of unpleasant feedback, so even a small child can be forced to part of this. That all I know, for example now, when she has been in the day care centre since August, she has been very well part of that group.*
(N1 Female)


No, on sitä nyt toki, mut vähän. Että meil on ollu semmonen periaate, et siihen puututaan heti. Ja tuolla koulussa, siel on myöski, siel on silleen opettajat ottanu sen niinku asiakseen. Niihin asioihin, mitä on ilmi tullu, ni niihin on heti puututtu. Ettei mitään lähetä silleen peittelemään tai niinku kiertelemään.
(N4 Mies)

*There is well that, but only a little. That we have got that kind of principle that we interfere that immediately. And there in school, also the teachers have been taken that as their mission. The things that have come out, they have immediately interfered. So nothing will be covered or circled.*
(N4 Male)


All the interviewees were very happy with the staff of their children's schools and day cares. One parent mentioned that the day care teacher has even specialized in multiculturalism. From the bases of the experiences of these interviewees it seems that the smaller children do not pay attention to each others ethnic background so much as the older ones. This may also explain why only the older adopted children have faced bullying because of their looks. Everyone but one parent told that in their children's day cares and schools there were children from many different ethnic backgrounds. Only one parent had noticed that other family's child's skin colour has been noticed among the children. Because the smaller children seem to be so open to all ethnicities, it would be interesting to how and why situation changes and bullying comes to picture when the children reach school age.

(...) ei oo päiväkodin lapset hirveesti kiinnittäny huomiota, et se on aika jännä, et joku raja menee ilmeisesti tässä ihonvärissä että, sen sijaan tää [vieraan lapsen nimi] joka on tää tummaihonen, ni afrotaustanen, ni hänen ihoonsa on kiinnitetty huomiota. (...)
(N5 Nainen)

*(...) the children in the day care centre have not paid so much attention, like it is quite interesting that some kind of line goes between skin colours, this [name of other than own child] instead, who has a dark skin, an African background, her skin has been paid attention to. (...)*
(N5 Female)

(...) ettei [lapsen nimi] suinkaan oo ainoo siellä päiväkodissa. Että siinä mielessä ihan hyvä. Hirveen hyvää on se päiväkotihenkilökunta, että kyl ne tota varmasti huomioi koko ajan ja pyrkii estämään kaikki kiusaamistilanteet ja puuttumaan niihin heti jos jotain semmosta on. (...)
(N1 Nainen)

*(...) so that [child's name] is not at all only in the day care centre. So in that way it is good. The staff in the day care centre is really good, so I am sure that they pay attention to it all the time and aim to prevent bullying and interfere them immediately if something like that occurs. (...)*
(N1 Female)

(...) No kyllä he on ainoot, et ei siellä muita ole. Että se on semmonen pieni koulu, siin on joku reilu kuutisenkymmentä oppilasta, kolmen opettajan koulu, et se on oikeestaan aika semmonen ihanteellinen, ihanteellisen kokonen koulu.
(N4 Mies)

*(...) Well they are the only ones, so there are no others. It is that kind of a small school with about 60 pupils and three teachers, so it is in a way that kind of an ideal sized school.*
(N4 Male)

(...) päiväkodissa missä [lapsen nimi] oli, ni siel oli semmonen opettaja joka oli tehny tämmöset monikulttuuriset opinnot tuolla yliopistolla ja se oli ollu Afrikassa harjottelemassa. Ja sit se sattu

jotenki niinku sen tilanteeseen aika hyvin, et sille tuli sellanen lapsi, joka sopi siihen hyvin. Ja se oli kauheen motivoitunu sitten, että pääs [lapsen nimi] tarpeet huomioon ja se oli hirveen hyvä vuosi onnistu oikein hyvin. (…)
(N4 Mies)

*(…) in the day care centre where [child's name] was, there was a teacher who had completed these kind of multicultural studies at the university, and she had been having her practical training in Africa. And it suited the situation really well that she got a child who was perfect for that. And it [the teacher] was really motivated, when she was able to make allowance for [child's name] needs, and it was a really good year, it succeed really well. (…)*
(N4 Male)

Even none of the parents reported any bullying of the children who were still at day care, bullying and racism were the issues that the parents carefully discussed at home. Usually the discussions dealt with people being different in general. This could relate to parents impressions of identity building. They do not want to highlight that some would be different because of the appearance, but that every person is unique, and no one is still better than the other. Of course parents know that their children understand that they do not look the same as the majority of Finns.

(…) Ja sit ollaan paljon puhuttu siitä, että ihmiset on erilaisia ja hyvä niin. Mut semmosta, että heihin saattas kohdistua jotain, (…) se tulee todennäkösesti täysin yllättäen, että vaikka sitä kuinka miettis ni se tulee varmaan erilaisessa tilanteessa esille, ku mitä, miten ehkä suunnittelee. (…) et niinku tän tyyppistä keskustelua ehkä pyrkii pitämään myöskin siitä näkökulmasta. Että voi olla joskus että heitä kiusataan.
(N5 Nainen)

*(…) And then we have talked a lot about the fact that people are different and that is a good thing. But about that something could be targeted to them (…) it will probably emerge as complete surprise, so that even how much you would think about it, so it will probably occur in a different situation than you have planned. (…) so we try to keep on this kind of conversation also from that point of view. So that it can be that they someday get bullied.*
(N5 Female)

(…) totta kai se sillain pidetään esillä ja normaalina asiana tavallaan sitäkin, että tota, että on toisen näkönen ku suomalaiset keskimäärin. Et se ei tietysti sitä suomalaisuutta mistään vähennä. (…)
(N3 Mies)

*(…) of course we have in the view, and as normal thing as well that [the child] looks different than Finnish people on average. And it does not lessen the Finnishness. (…)*
(N3 Male)

In two cases the parents were themselves active in bringing their children's ethnic background out in day cares. These included country and culture "theme days" where other children in the day cares were told about the roots of the adopted children. These parents of Chinese and Ethiopian children are in that sense more active than the others, but it can more likely be because of their personality than the country of adoption. Or probably these persons wanted to protect their children more, or just help their children's friends to understand that different birth culture is the reason why their children do not look like majority in the day care. It is sometimes said that people are afraid of the things that they do not understand, so getting knowledge about different cultures in early age could maybe help the children to grow up more open minded. Or at least appreciate their friend's exiting situation with two "home" countries.

*(…) et viime vuonna päiväkodissa oli Kiina-näytteet kiinalaisen uudenvuoden aikana. (…) et meillä oli niinku sitä koristetavaraa ihan uuteenvuoteen liittyen ja ihan niinku tämmösiä kiinalaisia tavaroita mitä meillä oli (…). (…) ni siin on sitte ihan useampi tunti käytetty aikaa siihen kiinalaiseen uuteenvuoteen ja meijän tytöt on ollu sit semmosena, niinkun niinku, kiinalaiseen uuteenvuoteen liittyen, et lapsille annetaan punasessa kirjekuoressa rahaa. Ni meil on ollu aidot tämmöset punaset Kiinasta hankitut kirjekuoret, johon me ollaan sitten laitettu hedelmärahaa. Että tytöt on niinku kahdella kädellä, niinku Kiinassa tavataan antaa ni antanu sit kaikille lapsille siellä päiväkodissa rahat (…).*
(N5 Nainen)
*(…) in last year we had in the day care centre China display during the Chinese New Year. (..) we had like decorations thing related to New Year and like this kinds of Chinese things what we had (…). (…) so there has then been several hours spent on the Chinese New Year, and our girls have been there like that kind of, like, like, what is related to the Chinese New Year is that children are given money in red envelope. So we have had these kinds of genuine red envelopes from China, and we put fruity candy coins inside them. So the girls, with two hands like they are accustomed to do in China, have given all the children in the day care centre the money (…).*
(N5 Female)

*(…) semmosen cd:n, mis oli paljon niinku amharan, niinku etiopialaisia lastenlauluja. (…) [lapsen nimi] meni sillon, oli ollu kolme viikkoo, kolme neljä viikkoo täällä, ku alko esikoulu ja se meni sitte samantien sinne esikouluun. Ja sinne me sit vietiin se cd ja kaikkea muuta semmosta tavaraa mitä meillä oli mukana. (…)*
(N4 Mies)
*(…) that kind of CD that included a lot like Amharan, like Ethiopian songs for children. (…) [child's name] went there, she had been three weeks, three, four weeks in here, when the pre-school begun and went there straight away. And we brought there that CD and all other kinds of things we had with us. (…)*
(N4 Male)

# 7. CONCLUSIONS

Like Lee (2003: 724) states: "there is a lack of a formal theory specific to transracial [international] adoptive families". I, anyhow, used and combined two of existing theories (Lee's theory and Vonk's theory and recommendations) that are specific to adoptive families. I found out that the most important skills these five Finnish international adoptive parents in this case study feel they need are:

1) The ability to accept how other people will react to a child that comes from different ethnic background.
2) The skills needed in surviving from racism.
3) The ability to "explain" the children to other.
4) Bonding with the child with unknown past experiences, and other the skills to go trough the adoption process itself.

Because the sample in the present study is small, my statements here can not be generalized to all Finnish international adoptive parents. However, in the light of my findings, the parents' age guides their choice in choosing the country of adoption; the factor that the research made in the United States did not bring up at all. The tight Finnish adoption laws may be one reason for that. Finnish adoptive parents also have to choose from the country options that all have their own limitations considering the parents, as in the United States even private adoptions are possible to arrange. Even the age limitations guided the choices of two interviewees, it does not mean that they would not have found the country they liked – they chose the ones that they had positive experiences of. The others told as well that their choice of country rose from their interest to the particular country and its culture. Or as in one case, the interest grew at least after the decision, when parents begun to learn about the country and its culture as much as possible. That shows that Finnish international adoptive parents in this study are active and eager to learn about their adoptive children's birth cultures.

The same eagerness also shows up in this research as Finnish adoptive parents consider the skills in ethnic awareness important and had also paid attention to the fact that they were going to adopt a child from different ethnic background and their feelings about being parent for that child. Even two of the interviewees said that they did not really consider people's ethnic background significant, they still have considered what reactions the child's ethnic background would cause in surrounding environment.

The interviewees named surviving racism the most important skill for international adoptive parents in Finland. This could have been read, not only from the straight questions about the needed skills, but also between the lines from how parents have considered their children's ethnic background before adoption, have asked their friends and relatives opinions, have given a thought to their place of residence, the way they talked about strangers' questions, and have discussed with their children about all people being different.

As also the previous research (Pitkänen 2000) showed, Finnish international adoptive parents are active in supporting their children's identity development. The ways and means for doing that are pretty much same as in Vonks recommendations, but in Finland the adopted children, at least according to the parents interviewed in this study, do not learn the language of their birth culture when they are still little.

In this study the parents left the issues of learning language to the future. The importance of adoptees' learning of their birth country's language would be a good subject for future academic research, because in learning the culture, language could be a bridge that helps to gain better understating for the culture and its concepts as well. That is why language can also be the worst barricade when you want to get into a new culture. If you do not know the language it is quite difficult to understand events completely. And vice versa, "language is the key to opening the culture's coffers of interrelationship and knowledge riches" (Seelye & Wasilewski 1996: 46). When two people speak the same language they can identify as belonging to a same group, but the similarity of general cultural milieu plays most often more important role in the experience. Still "fluency in common language provides a potential means to a shared identity" (Seelye & Wasilewski 1996: 48). So what is the effect that learning the language has in the adopted children's ability to internalize their birth culture, and does it have any function in identity building?

Finnish adoptive parents in this study did not, in the time of this research, have any contact with non-adopted adults or children from their children's birth country. So in this case, Vonk's thoughts about the importance that the adoptive families would have some contacts with people of their children's ethnic background in order to build pride in their ethnicity and/or birth culture, does not fulfil.

However, one interviewee told about a plan to participate the university's friendship program later, so the children would then meet a person(s) from their birth country. Two interviewees told that they are friends with people from other ethnic backgrounds. Music, food, books, toys, flags, discussions about the country, etc., were the ways how parents wanted to raise their children's awareness of their birth cultures.

The meaning of this research is not, however, to solve the dilemma that the parents can not teach their children about the culture to which they themselves do not belong (Steinberg and Hall 1998). And, as I stated earlier, the parents interviewed in this study did not even try to raise their children as Chinese or Ethiopian. They all told that they mainly raise their adopted children as Finns, according to "normal Finnish principles in raising the child".

According to my limited data, I would not place the Finnish international adoptive parents in any category that Lee has created. Vonk's categories, however, are applicable as Finnish adoptive parents seemed to understand the importance of all the skills presented in her theory. This study, however, revealed that Finnish international adoptive parents should have their own unique category that combines both: cultural socialization strategy and Vonk's theory of the skills that international adoptive parents need. The classification or category I now created, describes the Finnish adoptive parents in this study. It includes parts of all the categories that Lee presents, but it is impossible to place these Finnish parents, or even one parent interviewed, to one particular section of these categories. This proves that Lee's theory is not applicable to these Finnish international adoptive parents without modulation.

## 7.1 Guiding Half-Enculturation

The Finnish adoptive parents are ethnically aware, and these particular parents had even travelled a lot and lived abroad and that way also gotten familiar with different countries and cultures. Their decision of adopting a child from particular country seemed deliberate and they also understood what kind of difficulties the children from different ethnic background can face from the side of majority. This correlates to Vonk's requirements of ethnic awareness (Vonk 2001). These parents also learned the culture of their adopted children's birth country and celebrated it in their home via food, music, etc. They also attended groups of other international adoption families. The lack of this research is, that it does not reveal, if the parents chose to promote their children's ethnicities because they were aware of the earlier studies that correlated this kind of a function to positive identity development, or not. However, it seemed to be undisputed to them to do so. And this activity correlates to Vonk's multicultural planning. These Finnish adoption parents seemed to be well prepared for the racism that can be expressed toward their children. First this has crossed their minds already in the beginning of the adoption process. Surviving racism and strangers reactions was also the most important skill the interviewees think that Finnish adoption parents need. They also talked about the issue at home and discussed it with their children, which reveals that Finnish international adoptive parents are well equipped with the abilities Vonk requires for survival skills.

With reference to Lee's cultural socialization theory, I would like adapt it more suitable to Finnish adoptive parents by adding one more classification to it. As I mentioned earlier, according to my research data, it is impossible to fit Finnish adoptive parents into Lee's classifications. By the explanations through Vonk's requirements I presented above, it can be seen that the Finnish adoptive parents express parts of all Lee's cultural socialization categories. Strong influences of cultural assimilation are present, as parents want raise their children to become Finns. But if parents are not ethnically aware and they refuse to see any ethnic differences in their children, they are likely to use this strategy, which is not the case with Finnish parents, who have considered the ethnic differences with parents and children very carefully. Even that few of the Finnish parents showed slightly emphasis to ethnic inculcation, they did not really stand up in the community to promote social justice. Their ethnic inculcation was more stressed to prevent bullying of their own children by, for example, presenting their birth country and culture in the day care centres. This could be also seen in the answer dealing with immigrants; the parents did express neutral, if still slightly positive, opinion about immigrants. They did not, for example, bring up opinions that immigrants are discriminated, or anything that could refer to greater activity in the community with these issues. The child's choice was also present in the means that all the parents told that they did not want to "push" or force the birth culture to their adopted children. But still it was not only on their children's responsibility to learn about the culture, but parents brought up the subject time by time in "suitable situations". The closest classification for Finnish international adoptive parents would be the enculturation where parents are ethnically aware and provide their children with opportunities to instil ethnic pride. But, as I proved before, this is not enough as the parents also had features from the other three categories.

My suggestion here is that Finnish adoptive parents belong to category called: *Guiding half-enculturation*. It completes Lee's classifications in the way that it gives category for the *parents who mainly want to raise their internationally adopted children as Finns, but also want them to have an opportunity to know their roots and birth culture, but still are not forcing it*. In other words, they gently guide their children by providing the opportunities to get known their birth culture, but only within the limits that a person who have not lived in that culture can. If the children want to learn more about it when they are older (language, etc.), the parents will support them. These parents are also conscious of the existing of racism, and are willing to fight against it in their direct nearby environment, but do not take further communal actions.

7.2 International Adoptive Parents' Special Skills

To return once more to the other theory: not all the recommendations in Vonk's classification are important to, or suitable for Finnish international adoptive parents. My recommendations, that I named as *Special skills needed in international adoptive parenting* (modulated from Vonk's recommendations) for the future Finnish international adoptive parents, from the bases of the interview data, would be the following.

Special skills needed in international adoptive parenting are the ability to:

- Have thoroughly examined your motivation for adopting a child of a different ethnicity or culture than yourself.
- Examine your feelings and attitudes about the birth culture and ethnicity of your children.
- Be aware of the attitudes of friends and relatives toward your child's ethnic and cultural differences.
- Understand the unique needs of your child related to his or her ethnic or cultural status.
- Know that international-cultural adoptive parenting involves extra responsibilities over and

above those of biological parenting.
- Be prepared for the fact that strangers will ask you and your children questions about their ethnic background.
- Discuss with the child how to answer these questions.
- Understand that your children may be treated unkindly or unfairly because of racism.
- Discuss with your children about the realities of racism and discrimination.
- Continue to develop respect for the culture of your children's ethnic heritage and help your children develop pride in them selves.
- Provide your children with the opportunity to learn and appreciate their birth culture in the ways that you can offer him/her. This can include music, traditions or food of the birth culture, learning the language, reading books, visiting the birth country or participating cultural events, etc.

7.3 Discussion and Evaluation of the Study

The validity of the research means researches' ability to measure the thing it was meant to measure, or in this case describe. (Hirsijärvi et. al 2003: 213.) Validity in the qualitative research is improved when researcher gives an explicit coverage of the conducting of the research (Hirsijärvi et al. 2003: 214). In this research I have described precisely how the material has been gathered and analyzed and what kind phases these have included. I also present straight quotations from the interview data to support my analysis. The parents that have been interviewed are from different places down from Middle Finland, so the results are not tied to one place only geographically. This research gave answer to the research question, so the question proved to be successful. The question was "What kind of special skills these international adoptive parents feel they need in international adoptive parenting?" and the answer was presented earlier (see 7. Conclusions). The theoretical background was also suitable for this particular study in understanding the phenomenon. Because of these arguments, I consider the validity of this research good.

There can still be the question if five persons is enough to generalize these findings, and that is why I would recommend that the new category I created for Finnish international adoptive parents, would be tested empirically in a quantitative study with bigger amount of respondents. In this case study five parents were suitable enough, even their answers were pretty unanimous, and wider research could bring up more variations. The research would have been even more interesting, if I would have asked the parents deeper questions about their views of children's identity development.

This particular new category, the recommendations I created to Finnish adoptive parents, and all the findings of this study could be used as a helping tool for the future adoptive parents, maybe already during the counselling process. This research will hopefully also help to bring up some issues/skills with which the adoptive parents would need more help/information during the international adoption process.

The concepts of race and ethnicity rose up during this research, because some of the interviewees talked about their children's ethnicities and others about races. It would be interesting to see future research about the issues: can we talk about ethnicity with a person that grows up in a different culture than his/her birth culture? Is ethnicity about how someone looks or where he or/she feels to belong? This has been the habit widely around the world, even the concepts of race is same time present in some studies. Or should the terms ethnicity and race be replaced by the term "genetically induced varieties in human populations" as Seelye & Wasilewski prefer (1996: 38)?

BIBLIOGRAPHY:

Andujo E. (1988). *Ethnic Identity of Transethnically Adopted Hispanic Adolescents*. Social Work, No. 33, 531-535.

Cederblad M., Höök, B., Inhammar M., and Mercke, A. (1999). *Mental Health in International Adoptees as Teenagers and Young Adults: An Epidemiological Study*. Journal of Child Psychology & Psychiatry & Allied Disciplines, No. 40, 1239-1248.

DeBerry, K. M., Scarr, S., and Weinberg R. (1996). *Family Racial Socialization and Ecological Competence: Longitudinal Assessments of African-American Transracial Adoptees*. Child Development, No. 67, 2375-2399.

Del Pilar, J.A., and Udasco, J.O. (2004). *Marginality Theory: the Lack of Construct Validity*. Hispanic Journal of Behavioral Sciences, Vol. 26, No. 1, 3-15.

Eskola, J., and Suoranta, J. (1998). *Johdatus laadulliseen tutkimukseen*. Jyväskylä Gummerus.

Friedlander, Myrna L., Larney, Lucille C., Skau, M., Hotaling, M., Cutting M.L., and Schwam M. (2000). *Bicultural Identification: Experiences of Internationally Adopted Children and Their Parents*. Journal of Counseling Psychology, Vol. 47, No. 2, 2000, 187-198.

Haimi-Kaikkonen, A., Ojuva, A., and Kumpumäki T. (2006). *Kansainvälinen adoptio on haasteellinen prosessi*. Helsingin Sanomat, 31.12.2006.

Hall, S. (ed. & trans. Lehtonen M. & Herkman J.) (2002). *Identiteetti*. 4th edition. Tammerpaino Oy. Tampere.

Helsingin kaupunki, Sosiaalivirasto, Perheoikeudelliset asiat (2006). *Adoptio - lapseksiottaminen* (information package).

Hill, C. E., Thompson, B. J., and Williams, E. N. (1997). *A Guide to Conducting Consensual Qualitative Research.* The Counselling Psychologist, No. 25, 517-572.

Hirsijärvi, S., Remes, P., and Sajavaara P. (2003). *Tutki ja kirjoita.* $6^{th}$-$9^{th}$ edition. Dark Oy. Vantaa.

Hollingsworth, L. D. (1997). *Effect of Transracial/Transethnic Adoption on Children's Racial and Ethnic Identity and Self-Esteem: A Meta-Analyctic Review.* Marriage & Family Review, Vol. 25, 99-130.

Huh, N. S., and Reid W. K. (2000). *Intercountry, Transracial Adoption and Ethnic Identity.* International Social Work, Vol. 43, No. 1, 75-87.

Johson, P. R., Shireman, J. F, and Watson, K.W. (1987). *Transracial Adoption and the Development of Black Identity at Age Eight.* Child Welfare, Vol. 66, 45-55.

Kats, M., and Krank, A. (ed.) (1989). *Lapsemme ulkomailta. Kansainvälisestä adoptiosta.* Interpedian julkaisuja. Painokaari Oy. Helsinki.

Kerwin, C., Ponterotto, J. G., Jackson B. L, and Harris A. (1993). *Racial Identity in Biracial Children: A Qualitative Investigation.* Journal of Counselling Psychology, No. 40, 221-231.

Kim, Y. Y. (2001). *Becoming Intercultural : An Integrative Theory of Communication and Cross-Cultural Adaptation.* Thousand Oaks. Sage Publications.

Kivel, P. (1998). *White Benefits, Middle Class Priviledge.* In Cunnigham, S. and Bower, J.W. (ed.), Parenting Resource Manual. St. Paul, MN: North American Counsil on Adopted Children.

Laukkanen, E. (2007). *Olemme EU:n ulkomaalaisvastaisimpia.* Helsingin Sanomat. 21.1.2007.

LeComte, M. D., and Preissle, J. (1993). *Ethnography Qualitative Design in Educational Research.*

London. Academic Press

Lee, R. M. (2003). *The Transracial Adoption Paradox: History, Research, and Counseling Implications of Cultural Socialization.* The Counseling Psychologist, Vol. 31, No. 6, November 2003, 711-744.

McRoy, R. G., and Zurcher, L. A. (1983). *Transracial and Inracial Adoptees.* Springfiel IL. Charles Thomas.

Metsämuuronen, J. (2001). *Laadullisen tutkimuksen perusteet.* Metodologia-sarja 4. $2^{nd}$ edition. (painoa ei ilmoitettu) Viro.

Mikkola, P. (2001). *Kahden kulttuurin taitajaksi : maahanmuuttajaoppilaan monikulttuurinen identiteetti, tavoitteet ja toiminta.* Turun yliopiston julkaisuja. Sarja C, Scripta lingua Fennica Edita : osa 171. Turun yliopisto.

Padilla, Amado M. (2006). *Bicultural Social Development.* Hispanic Journal of Behavioral Sciences, Vol. 28, No. 4, November 2006, 467-497.

Park, R. E. (1928). *Human Migration and the Marginal Man.* American Journal of Sociology, Vol. 33, 881-893.

Parviainen, H. (2003). *Kansainvälinen adoptiotoiminta Suomessa vuosina 1970-2000.* Väestöntutkimuslaitoksen julkaisusarja E 15/2003. Väestöntutkimuslaitos. Väestönliitto. Hakapaino Oy. Helsinki.

Pitkänen, M. (2000). *Kansainväliset adoptiovanhemmat lapsen etnisen kulttuurin ja identiteetin tukijoina.* Pro gradu -työ. Helsinki. Helsingin yliopisto.

Pärssinen-Hentula, I. (1993). *Kansainvälisesti adoptoitujen lasten etninen identiteetti : haastattelututkimus adoptoitujen lasten suhteesta synnyinmaahansa.* Pro gradu -työ. Helsinki. Helsingin yliopisto.

Seelye, N. H., and Wasilewski, J. H., (1996). *Between Cultures : Developing Self-Identity in a world of Diversity.* Lincolnwood. NTC Publishing Group.

Silverman, A. R., (1993). *Outcomes of Transracial Adoption.* The Future of Children: Adoption, Vol. 3, No. 1, 104-108.

Steinberg, G., and Hall, B. (2000). *Inside Transracial Adoption.* Indianapolis, IN. Perspectives Press.

Tajfel, H. (edited by) (1982). *Social Identity and Intergroup Relations.* Cambridge. University Press.

Tessler, R., Gamache, G., and Liu, L. (1999). *West Meets East: Americans Adopt Chinese Children.* Westport, CT. Bergin & Garvey.

Uhtio, A. (2006). *Monikulttuurinen vai monirotuinen?* Adoptioperheet, No. 3, 2006, 42.

Van Gulden, H., and Bartels-Rabb, L. M. (2005). *Real parents, real children: parenting the adopted child.* New York. The Crossroad Publishing Company.

Virkki, H. (2006). *Suomalaisuuden monet kasvot - pro gradu tutkielma kansainvälisesti adoptoiduista nuorista.* Adoptioperheet, No. 3, 2006, 12-13.

Vonk, E. M. (2001). *Cultural Competence for Transracial Adoptive Parents.* Social Work, Vol. 46, No. 3, July 2001, 246-255.

Wickens, K. L., and Slate, J. R. (1996). *Transracial Adoption of Koreans: A Preliminary Study of Adjustment.* International Journal for the Advancement of Counselling, Vol. 19, 187-195.

Westues, A., and Cohen, J. S. (1998). *Racial and Ethnic Identity of Internationally Adopted Adolescents and Young Adults: Some Issues In Relation to Children's Rights.* Adoption Quarterly, Vol. 1, 33-55.

Yoon, D. P. (2001). *Causal Modeling Predicting Psychological Adjustment of Korean-Born Adolescent Adoptees.* Journal of Human Behavior in the Social Environment, Vol. 3, 65-82.

INTERNET RESOURCES:

Adoptioperheet ry, 2006. *Laki lapseksiottamisesta 8.2.1985/153.* Cited 30.4.2006.
http://www.adoptio.org

Adoptioperheet ry, no date. *Adoptiosta.* Cited 21.10.2006.
http://www.adoptioperheet.fi/tietoa_adoptiosta.html

Dick, B. (2005). *Grounded theory: a thumbnail sketch.* Cited 24.1.2007.
http://www.scu.edu.au/schools/gcm/ar/arp/grounded.html

Encyclopedia of Adoption, 2000. *Transracial adoption.* Cited 1.11.2006.
http://encyclopedia.adoption.com/entry/transracial-adoption/360/1.html

Freundlich, M., and Lieberthal, J. K. (2000). *The Gathering of the First Generation of Adult Korean Adoptees: Adoptees' Perceptions of International Adoption.* Cited 23.1.2007.
http://www.adoptioninstitute.org/proed/korfindings.html

Hautala, S. (2007). *Etnografia.* Cited 8.3.2007.
http://www.uta.fi/laitokset/hoito/wwwoppimateriaali/luku5h.html

Suomen kansainvälisten lapseksiottamisasioiden lautakunta. *Toimintakertomus 2004, 2005:8.* Cited 29.10.2006. http://www.stm.fi/Resource.phx/publishing/store/2005/09/hl1125662884635/passthru.pdf

Tilastokeskus. *Adoptiot.* Cited 30.4.2006.
http://www.tilastokeskus.fi/til/adopt/index.html

Tilastokeskus, updated 16.6.2006. *Suomeen adoptoitu ulkomailta lapsia ennätysmäärä vuonna 2005.* Cited 21.10.2006. http://www.stat.fi/til/adopt/2005/adopt_2005_2006-06-16_tie_001.html

APPENDIX 1.

THEMES IN THEME INTERVIEWS

The Family History
- Details of the adopted child (age when adopted, country where from adopted)
- Reasons for choosing a specific country for adoption.

About Ethnicity
- Have you considered if your own cultural/ethnic background effects the way you are going to raise your child? How?
- What kind of thoughts you have/have had about the immigrants?
- What kind of experiences did you have from your child's native culture before adoption?
- Did you study that culture? How? Have you visited in your child's birth country before adoption?
- What was your reason for adopting a child of a different ethnicity or culture than yourself?

Skills Needed in International Adoptive Parenting

- Do you think that your child has unique needs related to his or her ethnic or cultural status? What kind of they are?
- Do you think that international-cultural adoptive parenting involves skills over and above those of biological parenting? What kinds of?
- Have you thought and/or experienced that others may view your family as "different"?

Supporting the Child's Birth Culture
- Are you telling your child about the culture of his/her ethnic heritage?
- Do you have friends from that culture or another contact to people from the culture?
- Have you developed friendships with families and individuals from other cultures?
- Do you purchase books, toys, and dolls that are from child's birth country?
- Do you include traditions from your child's birth culture in your family celebrations?

- Do you provide your children with the opportunity to appreciate the music of their birth culture?
- Do you know any adults from your children's birth culture?
- Does the child her/himself ask about her/his birth country/culture? What kind of questions?

### Issues of Racism

- Are there other children from different ethnic background in your children's school or day care centre?
- Do you think if your choices about where to live affect your child?
- Have you thought that your children may be treated unkindly or unfairly because of racism?
- Do you tell your children about the realities of racism and discrimination?
- Do you help your children cope with racism through open and honest discussion in our home about race and oppression?
- What kinds of attitudes your friends and family members have/had toward your child's ethnic differences?
- Has your child had attempts to alter his/her physical appearance to look more like family members or friends? How did you solve the situation?
- Do you help your children develop pride in them selves? How?
- Has the children been bullied because of their ethnic or adoption background?
- Have you given the children practical information about how to deal with insensitive questions from strangers? What is you advice?

### About The Native Language

- Do your children learn the language of their birth culture?
- Did parents speak that language before they adopted the child?
- Or learn it afterwards/or speak it at all?

www.ingramcontent.com/pod-product-compliance
Lightning Source LLC
Chambersburg PA
CBHW071413290426
44108CB00014B/1803